Masculine Identity
in Hardy and Gissing

Masculine Identity in Hardy and Gissing

Annette Federico

Rutherford ● Madison ● Teaneck
Fairleigh Dickinson University Press
London and Toronto: Associated University Presses

Associated University Presses
440 Forsgate Drive
Cranbury, NJ 08512

Associated University Presses
25 Sicilian Avenue
London WC1A 2QH, England

Associated University Presses
P.O. Box 39, Clarkson Pstl. Stn.
Mississauga, Ontario
L5J 3X9 Canada

The paper used in this publication meets the requirements
of the American National Standard for Permanence of Paper
for Printed Library Materials Z39.48-1984.

Library of Congress Cataloging-in-Publication Data

Federico, Annette, 1960–
   Masculine identity in Hardy and Gissing / Annette Fedrico.
      p.   cm.
   Includes bibliographical references and index.
   ISBN 0-8386-3423-0 (alk. paper)
   1. English fiction—19th century—History and criticism.
   2. English fiction—Men authors—History and criticism.   3. Hardy,
   Thomas, 1840–1928—Knowledge—Psychology.   4. Gissing, George,
   1857–1903—Knowledge—psychology.   5. Masculinity (Psychology) in
   literature.   6. Identity (Psychology) in literature.   7. Men in
   literature.   I. Title.
   PR878.M45F43   1991
   832'.809353—dc20   90-56171
                                                       CIP

PRINTED IN THE UNITED STATES OF AMERICA

To My Parents

Contents

Introduction   13
1. Masculine Identities   18
2. Nasty Boys: *The Emancipated* and *In the Year of
   Jubilee*   29
3. Pathological Gentlemen: *Far from the Madding Crowd*
   and *The Woodlanders*   55
4. Modern Romantics: *The Well-Beloved* and *The Odd
   Women*   76
5. The Other Victim: *Jude the Obscure* and *The Whirlpool*   102
Conclusion   130

Notes   136
Works Cited   143
Index   147

Acknowledgments

Acknowledgment is due to William Siebenschuh for his guidance, encouragement, and discerning criticism at each stage of this project. I am also grateful to Jim Zimmerman for his talent at counterpoising seriousness and good fun in many conversations about books and life.

Masculine Identity
in Hardy and Gissing

Introduction

Many recent critical works deal with issues of gender and the novel, and many more social, historical, and psychological studies concentrate on gender and culture. Female sexuality and the role of women in society are understandably the usual focus of such studies, since women historically have been either disenfranchised and undervalued as literary and social agents, or else narrowly described from a strictly male point of view that, at various times, has been prim and perverse.

To explore men's imaginative rendering of the feminine is certainly an essential contribution to gender-based criticism. Recent studies of art and iconography (Bram Dijkstra's *Idols of Perversity* [1986] and Jan Marsh's *Pre-Raphaelite Women* [1987], offer pervasive evidence of the late nineteenth-century male painter's antagonistic and fetishistic attitude toward women; Sandra Gilbert's and Susan Gubar's *No Man's Land* (1988–89) provides feminist literary critics with a fine analysis of male misogyny fueled by the ongoing debate over "the woman question" at the turn of the century; and in *Sexual Anarchy* (1990) Elaine Showalter finds compelling connections between gender in the culture of the fin de siècle and in the culture of the 1990s. Works in other disciplines, notably Peter Gay's two-volume study, *The Bourgeois Experience: Victoria to Freud* (1984–86), are valuable resources for the student of late nineteenth-century art, literature, and culture who is particularly interested in images of women and ideas about sex from the more powerful, socially legitimate male point of view.

However, outside of recent studies on homosexual literature (Eve Kosofsky-Sedgewick's *Between Men* and also Gregory Woods's *Articulate Flesh*) or social and historical research on the male image (J. A. Mangan's and James Walvin's collection of essays, *Manliness and Morality*), sustained analyses of male representation in novels by men has been a practice largely neglected by feminist and gender-based critics. The volatile nature of the culture's sense of masculinity toward the end of the century makes a study of male representation by men especially

13

compelling and informative; the subject of male characterization in fiction is open to interpretations broader than the function of male homoerotic desire in the novel or the self-projecting male ego recasting itself in fictions of sex and power. Working at a time crowded with debates about sexology and suffrage, and the possibilities of equality and love, the male novelist of the 1880s and 1890s created male characters who are structured in ambivalence, who are unable to escape consciousness of their sex or their awareness of changing definitions of masculinity in their society, and who are unable to conceal their anxiety about the increasing power of women. Troubled and aware of shifting sexual roles at the turn of the century, the male novelist may invent men who are in the process of self-invention, just as women writers of the same period describe female characters who are in the process of becoming liberated. To closely explore masculine characterization can do much to illuminate the sexual dynamics of the 1880s and 1890s, and perhaps equally important, may help to broaden a field of literary study that has so far concentrated almost solely on the representation of women. The inescapable ambivalence of same-sex characterization is like using a trick mirror to see what Virginia Woolf calls "the spot the size of a shilling on the back of the head," that part of our sexual selves we cannot know but for the studious eye of the sexual other. If we look at men's novels for the mirror-representation of a masculine self, instead of for the more manageable and distinct feminine other, we are bound to find distortions no less interesting and informative of cultural preoccupations than those distorted images of women that scholars have so assiduously pointed out.

The subtle problems confronting a man—the traditional bearer of the pen—when he invents another man—the traditional axis of fiction—certainly present new issues worth our attention. I should point out, however, that my particular interest here is less an examination of the late-century novelist's built-in schizophrenia when writing about male characters than an analysis of the types of male representation themselves. In other words, I have chosen to focus upon the tales, not the tellers.

Still, given that masculine characterization is a useful subject, especially in the late nineteenth century, why Thomas Hardy and George Gissing particularly? Outside of my admiration for Hardy's and Gissing's works, my first criterion in choosing these authors is their status as popular late-century English novelists who work in the realist tradition. It is not my concern here to look overmuch at male representation in the fantasy and adventure fiction of the 1880s and 1890s—Kipling, H. Rider Haggard, Bram Stoker, Robert Louis Stevenson—although I occasionally find instructive parallels between these authors and Hardy and Gissing. It is also not my point to make purely aesthetic judgments, although certainly I find Hardy's and Gissing's novels artistically more complete and satisfying than much of the other popular fiction of the day dealing with similar themes, and overall I feel their novels are not only expertly plotted in most cases, but often poetically expressive, finely conceived in terms of character and place, and intensely, sometimes movingly, true. I think Gissing's novels—praised by Virginia Woolf in 1912 as possessing the essential qualities of "life and completeness"— certainly deserve rereading and renewed study, as much for their somber realism as for their stylistic merits. But leaving aside the question of aesthetic value, Hardy's and Gissing's novels interest me most for their thematic profundity, their complex and serious approach to the problem of sexual identity, and their noticeable ambivalence in their treatment of masculine character.

Most critics agree that Hardy's women characters are more attractive, more memorable than his men, and virtually the only novel by Gissing that has been studied by feminist critics in recent years is *The Odd Women,* a novel with complex, articulate women characters who confront sexual inequality with candor and with courage. The critical attention given to Hardy's and Gissing's strong representations of women is justified, of course, but it is also somewhat exclusive. If Hardy's men seem less interesting than his women, it may be because of the novelist's ambivalent attitude toward male portraiture. He may know what kind of woman fascinates him (capricious, innocent, beautiful ones, mostly), but he is less certain about his male saints and seducers, those characters who always seem slightly uncomfortable with their roles in the novel. Similarly, Gissing's misogyny is well defined in most of his portrayals of women, from the nags to the viragos to the gentle martyrs, but his masculism is always unbalanced and qualified. His male characters are invariably egomaniacs, and yet so pleading, so frail: that is, modern day patriachs whose feelings are easily hurt.

I realize what a big subject issues of sexuality and the self or gender and personality present, and it is not my intention to explore the metaphysics of Self and Other, or sophistical notions of heroism. But inherent in the value of Hardy's and Gissing's novels is their capacity to explore how notions of masculine identity were beginning to evolve from the solid, monolithic patriarchal role of the mid-1800s to more malleable, less confident styles of manhood. I use the word "style" advisedly to suggest the troubled self-consciousness of some men at this period, who felt the need to keep up with changing expectations of masculinity, and often reached for a well-worn male stereotype to adopt instead of exploring the complicated emotions that constitute developing personalities. Masculine *identity* in these novels is thus in a state of crisis: the dynamic self, the unique and animated psyche of the male character, is suspended at a crucial point of change. Characters use reliable masculine *roles* as a substitute for the genuine and troublesome "New Man," whose needs and fears are often even more baffling to himself than are those of the formidable New Woman.

Throughout this book, I use Hardy's and Gissing's novels to help me to understand certain cultural ideas about the nature of masculinity, and I use four male roles, or stereotypes, to help me to identify those ideas in each of the eight novels I discuss. I need to emphasize that I use these roles to make my approach to male characterization in each novel manageable and coherent, and also as a means of recreating the cultural climate of the late nineteenth century or of talking about patriarchal attitudes in general. As I have stated, my central interest is more in close readings of the texts themselves than in a sustained examination of these particular stereotypes.

I have chosen the two opposite roles of the virile man and the chaste man, or the seducer and the saint, partly because they are evocative of the feminine madonna/magdalen division, but also because of Hardy's and Gissing's striking representations of both male roles. The third stereotype is the idealist, the romantic fantasizer who seeks the woman of his dreams—certainly the fiction of the age pandered to men's nostalgic fantasies, as well as to their fears of New Women. Opposite the fantasizer is the fourth type, the realist, who recognizes the presence of the New Woman and must try to deal with her as practically as he can.

My chapter divisions are based upon these four male stereotypes. Each focuses upon two novels as specific and striking manifestations of some aspect of masculine ideology as outlined above. In chapter 2, I look at *The Emancipated* and *In the Year of Jubilee* (Reuben Elgar's sexual urgency and Lionel Tarrant's mistaken seduction) as evidence of the late-century cult of virility and aggression, contrasted in *Far from the Madding Crowd* (Boldwood's suppressed virility) and *The Woodlanders* (Giles Winterborne's painfully chaste courtship) with the tradition of chivalry and sexual postponement, the subject of chapter 3. Chapters 4 and 5 are similarly structured companion studies: male sexual fantasy is set against a background of conservative and vulgar realism in two apparently dissimilar novels, *The Well-Beloved* and *The Odd Women* (Pierston's commonplace angels and Barfoot's more up-to-date intellectual); and the tranquil pleasures of love, commitment, and family compete with a whirlpool of feminist agitation and a chaos of moral principles in *Jude the Obscure* and *The Whirlpool* (Jude's acceptance of feminine "sex education," and Harvey Rolfe's retreat from female reality). The seducer, the saint, the idealist, and the practical man are four aspects of masculine identity I find most striking in Hardy and Gissing, and these comprise the rationale for my organization, as well as for my choice of the individual novels that ground the discussions in each chapter.

I should add that these four types of masculine identity were chosen because they seemed to me an efficient way to approach the difficult issue of male novelists who create a "male other." I did not invent these roles; I only recognized their fascinating presence in the works of two realistic late nineteenth-century writers. Certainly the types persist outside of these particular novels and outside of that particular period as well, as men continue to struggle to establish a genuine identity beyond the confines of patriarchal roles.

1

Masculine Identities

Both Hardy and Gissing dramatize the tensions in Victorian masculinity by describing men who are emotionally and psychologically entrapped by the roles they impose upon themselves. The extent to which male characters in their novels are consistently antagonized by their own obsessions suggests that both authors sensed the insufficiency of the various contemporary masculine codes of behavior, while at the same time they remained constrained by an extremely tenacious and time-honored interpretation of masculinity that rests on the notion of male superiority and the objectification of women. Therefore many male characters in the novels—especially the later works—attempt to reinterpret or reconstruct the sexual ideology that is their legacy, to, in effect, self-consciously declare themselves modern "versions" of some aspect of Victorian masculine identity. Late-century British culture provides the stereotypes against which each male protagonist aligns himself. Hardy and Gissing show how the romanticized image of the masculine self either self-destructs, or is overmatched by the complexities of unique personalities functioning in unique—often parlous—circumstances. They let their characters try on masculine poses in a "laboratory" setting that is the fictional world of the novel, and then watch the role gradually break down.

The nature of these masculine roles is dialectic, that is, intrinsically oppositional, and the pervasive sense not merely of contrasts but of imbalances, which informs novels such as *The Woodlanders* and *The Well-Beloved* or Gissing's *The Emancipated* and *In the Year of Jubilee,* is anchored in the precarious social and historical situation in which Hardy and Gissing lived and wrote. The state of the economy and the political events of the 1880s and 1890s—years Fraser Harrison describes as "fraught with turmoil and anxiety"[1]—were frighteningly unstable, and in their public roles, men began to feel gradually overwhelmed, sucked into the whirlpool of financial risk and imperialist con-

troversy. Their personal lives were perhaps even more tu-
multuous, as relationships with women became complicated by
"new ideas," feminist challenges to masculine "old ideas" (the
double standard, for instance), and a latent uneasiness with gender roles as defined by their society. The "Woman Question" was
ubiquitous, and the "Women's Movement" had begun to gather
tremendous momentum by about 1882, when the Married
Women's Property Act was passed twenty-six years after it had
been introduced into Parliament.[2] Other important issues
worked their way into legislation at about this time: two Matrimonial Causes Acts in 1882 and 1893 gave wives a legal identity
independent of their husbands, and the Maintenance of Wives
Act of 1886 protected working-class wives from desertion and
complete destitution. Equally important was the introduction of
birth control literature to middle-class wives, which significantly
altered women's attitudes toward their sexuality and their conjugal "duties." Educational opportunities for women were expanded from 1879, when London University offered all degrees
to women, and in 1886 when Oxford and Cambridge permitted
women to attend lectures and earn degrees. One of the most
important feminist achievements was the repeal of the Con-
tagious Diseases Acts (laws that forced prostitutes to undergo
examinations for veneral diseases for the protection of their "respectable" clients), passed without parliamentary debate in
1864, 1866, and 1869. Abolitionists, led by Josephine Butler,
carried on a dramatic and militant battle until the Acts were
finally repealed in 1886, proving that women could have a voice
in the male world of politics and power.

All of these quantifiable changes contributed to the ferment of
ideas about sexual relations and the nature of the sexes, provoking men to meditate upon their patriarchal inheritance. At the
end of the century, contradictory strands of middle-class attitudes still existed, and contributed to the tenuous construct of
Victorian masculinity.

Victorian sexual ideology has been widely documented, and
despite a patriarchal, objectively detached focus on "Woman" as
sexual other (as "the problem"), masculine ideology comes
across in these studies as something equally problematic.[3] Therefore, I have tried to separate particular strands from this large
ideological fabric by isolating specific masculine tendencies and
exploring their representations in selected novels by two authors
I find compelling both in their realistic (in Gissing's case almost
naturalistic) portrayals of late-Victorian life and thought, and in

their perhaps unconscious translations of a deeply felt sexual nervousness from the masculine point of view. Leaving aside for now the question of authorial intention and invitations to psychoanalyze the personality behind the text, it seems the cultural framework within which Hardy and Gissing wrote, combined with their experience as men—an inside view of "the reality experienced by the oppressors"[4]—intrinsically shapes their literary imaginations. Because I interpret the novels, even the less obvious "problem-novels" of the eighties and nineties, as functioning as both social and literary discourse, I have tried to prevent the social and cultural background from abstracting itself. Ideological values are present in Hardy's and Gissing's portraits of men, and we need only to identify appropriate terminology in which to organize and contrast these values. Hardy's and Gissing's patriarchal inheritance—their sense of masculine identities—is not alien or remote from the framework of modern western culture, and the four aspects of stereotypic masculinity that characterize their thinking are identifiable, indeed familiar. They are the virile man, the chaste man, the fantasizer, and the realist.

Not surprisingly, there are related interpretations of masculinity in the fiction and essays of Hardy's and Gissing's contemporaries, particularly George Meredith, who is considerably less panic-stricken by the sexual revolution. Unlike Meredith (*The Chronicle* for July 1895 grouped him with Hardy and Gissing as the three most important novelists of the day), Hardy and Gissing create male characters who are really almost mythical, in two senses of that word. They are "types" who appeal to the consciousness of a particular people and embody the ideals of a culture, and they are "fictions" or half-truths that form part of that culture's ideology. Where in Meredith, a character like Lord Fleetwood (in *The Amazing Marriage*, published 1895) is offered as an example of the self-styled aristocratic sporting male and examined with detached irony and slight contempt, in Hardy and Gissing, male characters who adopt futile poses are viewed with a mixture of helpless ambivalence, defensiveness, or regret. Their characters are less Meredithian examples of real men in English society than they are impersonators of a particular social myth. Thus, a character like Giles Winterborne can function as the "hero" of *The Woodlanders*, representing the chivalric myth, and at the same time can expose the uneasy falsification of the role he imposes upon himself. Likewise, Everard Barfoot in *The Odd Women* is a self-mythologized "modern man" who reverts to orthodoxy without even understanding the superficiality of his liberal pose. Despite even the apparent perversity of characters like Reuben Elgar, Alec d'Urberville, or Jocelyn Pierston, to take only three examples, they manage still to function as rein-terpretations of male roles they self-consciously adopt, which, in the realistic settings of their novels, seem perfectly tenable be-cause they are embedded in Victorian culture and society and in the psychology of male authors who are part of that society. In this sense, the masculine situations or identities manifested in men's virility or chastity, in their sexual fantasies and in the social reality, document and comment on the tension experi-enced by many Victorian men in the last two decades of the century.

Despite their apparent uneasiness with their society's pre-dominant constructions of masculinity, Victorian men, not ex-cluding Gissing and Hardy, were firmly entrenched in patriarchal assumptions. In *The Limits of Masculinity*, Andrew Tolson ex-plains how the notion of paternal inheritance can become rooted in men's personalities:

> He can invoke the ancient law of "patriarchy": the continuing sym-bolic power associated with property and inheritance, the organiza-tion of the family, and the maintenance of male supremacy. This history is truly "hidden," not only because it is largely unexamined by historians, but also because it enters into the present uncon-sciously—in cultural predispositions beneath the surface of individ-ual awareness. (1977, 14)

Thus although the masculine experience is cultural, social, and historical—"There is no 'universal' masculinity, but rather a varying masculine experience of each succeeding social epoch" (Tolson 1977, 13)—in Western civilization it is inextricably con-nected with work, property, and power. These perceived priv-ileges form the ideological husk outside the more distinct social definitions of what it meant to be a man in the time Hardy and Gissing lived and wrote.

The Victorian's sense of masculinity is constructed from con-tradictions, most of which evolve from a social attitude toward sexuality that is manifestly confused and insecure. The long held opinion that the Victorians were reticent about sex has since been convincingly refuted by Eric Trudgill, Ronald Pearsall, Ste-ven Marcus, and most recently Peter Gay, among others. In *Sex, Politics, and Society*, Jeffrey Weeks says that "far from being simply denied in the nineteenth century, sex acquired a peculiar significance in structuring ideology and political practices, and in shaping individual responses" (1981, 21). Male responses especially were studiously analyzed in scientific works such as William Acton's *Functions and Disorders of the Reproductive Organs* (first published in 1857), and either bolstered or proscribed in various manuals and handbooks, so that in many Victorian texts about male sexuality "self-help and self-abuse seem indistinguishable."[5] The severity of sexual repression in Victorian England is well-documented. Guilt associated with sex resulted in young boys' self-mutilation, monstrous antimasturbation contraptions, and violent homophobia, as well as in a completely polarized idea of women as either madonnas or magdelens—an image, as we know, reinforced by Victorian culture in the interest of policing the sexual psychologies of both men and women. Weeks describes how "many men battled valiantly with what they conceived of as temptation," the result being "a pitiable alienation of a whole class of men from their own sexuality" (Marcus 1964, 18).

A good fictional example of men's sexual alienation is in Samuel Butler's *The Way of All Flesh*, which despite its anti-Victorian preachiness, is a tolerably candid treatment of nineteenth-century masculine sexual repression and patriarchal tyranny over three generations. Devout young Ernest Pontifex is the product of institutionalized suppression and ignorance:

> it was ere long a still greater [shock] to find that certain thoughts which he had warred against as fatal to his soul, and which he had imagined he should lose once and for all on ordination, were still as troublesome to him as they had been; he also saw plainly enough that the young gentlemen who formed the circle of Pryer's friends were in much the same unhappy condition.
>
> This was deplorable. The only way out of it that Ernest could see was that he should get married at once.[6]

Though by no means innocently pious in sexual matters, Gissing could certainly have sympathized with such feelings of guilt and desperation—he was more than once tempted to pick up a work-girl in the streets to come live with him out of "desperate physical need," regardless of intellectual compatability.[7] Though many of the characters in his novels are more aggressive than Ernest Pontifex, they too are psychologically intimidated by a code of male chastity and see themselves as "victims" of their sex drives.

Although male sexual desire was soberly pushed under-
ground—"prudence and postponement" were the catchwords of
the bourgeoisie—the ideology of masculinity, or "Christian manliness," was enthusiastically erected. "Competitiveness, personal
ambition, social responsibility, and emotional restraint" are ele-
ments of the model "gentleman" (Tolson 1977, 39). It is will
power and self-reliance that define manliness, or as David Pugh
puts it in his work on nineteenth-century American men, "direct
action, rather than thoughtful consideration, was the best response to almost any situation. . . . Men could be measured not
by their deepest motivations, but by what they did based on
those motivations."[8] Paradoxically, the men in Gissing—Elgar,
Tarrant, Barfoot—do in fact measure themselves based on their
motivations, not on their accomplishments. They play the part of
the *artiste manqué* in search of "life," replacing the vulgarity of
work in the marketplace—a bourgeois definition of masculinity
based on commercial success—with purely mental occupations.
The ethic of male work remains intact for them, but they do not
have to dirty their hands. Thus in their reinterpretations of the
masculine role they assume they are paragons of manliness,
always busy with art, ideas, life. Toward 1890, in fact, "Life"
became a key word for many novelists and social thinkers. In *The
Edwardian Temperament*, Jonathan Rose describes the various
implications and meanings of the word as it was used even into
the twentieth century:

> It could mean the surrogate religion of vitalism, the worship of the
> life process as a spiritual force. It could specifically mean the crea-
> tion of new life, an erotic impulse breaking out of Victorian con-
> straints and sometimes worshipped as a religion in itself. Life could
> also be a mysterious spiritual quality that endowed human beings
> with identity, consciousness, a moral sense, and free will. . . . In its
> most general sense, life represented a demand for individual freedom
> and self-realization, a vague but fervent rallying cry for the poets,
> social rebels, and emancipated women who were fighting their way
> out of the drawing rooms.[9]

Twentieth-century writers, though, might have described sincere
seekers of "Life" with more affirmative attitudes as questers after
a truth that really could not exist in the drawing rooms—Lawrence, Forster, Conrad, Butler, and Huxley tend that way in many
of their novels. Hardy's and especially Gissing's designation of
the term, as applied to restless young Englishmen, is considerably more ambivalent. When these characters use "life" as a

slogan, or "experience" as a pop-cultural mantra, their motives and their real masculinity become suspect because the words are employed merely as part of a self-protective pose.

The notion of masculine action is naturally opposed to feminine "contemplation" or submissiveness, a further revision of the aggressive male/passive female theory that found so much support in scientific studies, such as Havelock Ellis's *Men and Women* (1894), and in eugenic theories that view both sexes as "breeders," biologically determined complements. Weeks refers to the flood of handbooks on how to achieve male self-sufficiency, and the inevitable problems men experienced in trying to live up to standards of virility—supported by biological principles—propounded by men like Ellis and Acton, who wrote that "its existence, indeed, seems necessary to give a man that consciousness of his dignity, of his character as head and ruler, and of his importance, which is absolutely essential to the well being of the family, and through it, of society itself" (quoted in Marcus 1964, 26). As protectors of the social order, men had a tremendous responsibility. Not surprisingly, sex in the middle classes was firmly policed, especially among adolescents. Public school training became decidedly militaristic. "From the 1860s there was a new cult of masculinity . . . Thomas Arnold's emphasis on spiritual autonomy and intellectual maturity was increasingly replaced by a new stress on physical characteristics, on the demonstration of pure willpower" (Weeks 1981, 40). Pierce Egan, Thomas Hughes, Charles Kingsley, and the manly heroes of Waterloo and Balaclava became masculine ideals—"Trollope's manly lovers and Dickens's manly aristocrats and mechanics all help to democratize and domesticate the traditional notion of chivalry with its associations of dedicated courage, loyalty, unselfish devotion and protection of the weak."[10]

The underside of repression and the chivalric ideal, however, is revealed in the fact that in 1850 there were at least fifty thousand prostitutes known to police in England and Scotland, eight thousand in London alone.[11] In an article on "Male Chastity in the Nineteenth Century" (*Contemporary Review*, November 1971), Gordon Haight cites a journal entry of Ralph Waldo Emerson's after his visit to London in 1848: "Carlyle and Dickens replied that chastity in the male sex was as good as gone in our times; and in England was so rare that they could name all the exceptions" (252). To be manly, Haight illustrates, does not necessarily mean to be pure, and in fact upper-class men had little respect for women of the lower ranks, who were considered fair game when it came to gathering requisite male "experience." To be courageous, honest, and tolerably truthful does not mean men were not also encouraged to "look about them."

This complicated and contradictory myth of masculinity was as much a prison as a privilege. The manliest of men were often seized with anxieties about masturbation, homosexuality, and their sexual desire for women—both the angels and the *femme fatales*. The promise of economic success and social status suggested by notions of duty and discipline was accompanied by threats and fears about failure. Economic depression between 1873 and 1896 sapped middle-class morale and contributed to men's increasing sense of insecurity, but even more dangerous to masculine assumptions of superiority was feminist agitation. Fraser Harrison discusses "the prevailing atmosphere of fearfulness" in the final three decades of the century:

> By the late 'eighties and 'nineties, women had decisively demonstrated that, however fiercely the march of emancipation might be resisted by men and by those traditionalists among women who chose to defend the mid-Victorian position . . . the era of female submissiveness was on the decline and waning fast. The cumulative effect of this bewildering, and often humiliating, revolution was to induce in men a profound sense of fear. This fearfulness was involved in acute apprehension concerning their capacity to withstand the "new woman's" aggression, as they saw it, and an intense dread of the new, and previously inaccessible dimension to sexuality that was being introduced by women who were no longer content to confine their role to that of the willing or unwilling victim of male rapacity, but who were now yearning for the chance to participate in sexual relations on equal emotional terms with their husbands (1978, 118).

Many men of course welcomed women's efforts for equality. Even Gissing, whose sympathy with feminism was by no means absolute, wrote in a letter to Eduard Bertz, "I am convinced there will be no social peace until women are intellectually trained very much as men are. More than half the misery of life is due to the ignorance and childishness of women." In other words, women's education was important if only to give men peace. Women's general excavation of their own suppressed desires helped unearth men's sexuality as well—instincts and drives they thought best suppressed and forgotten were beginning to be viewed by men "as a dimension of their nature that held exhilarating promise" (Harrison 1978, 133).

This is to fill out very briefly the social, cultural, and historical background that influenced the literary achievements of Hardy and Gissing, and that I will necessarily expand in separate discussions of the novels themselves. The feminist movement did more than generate subjects for these authors to write about. Heightened awareness of their own sexuality and of the current definitions of masculinity—especially the conflicts between virility and chastity (the separation of flesh and spirit that is central in Hardy), and the futility of male sexual fantasy in an increasingly feminist reality—informs their novels with a characteristic ambivalence that manifests itself in their portraits of men (though I need to emphasize that women in most of the novels are absolutely pivotal). The end of the nineteenth century brought private sexual experience into the realm of public dialogue. The effect of this exposure of a man's "secret life" took various forms in fact and in fiction. Declan Kiberd traces the evolution of what he calls "the self-doubting new man" in modern fiction, identifying the male response to the sexual revolution as ranging from Strindberg's "despair," Ibsen's and Hardy's "qualified optimism," and the "fearless exploration of new manhood and new womanhood" in Yeats, Lawrence, and Joyce.[12] Kiberd's discussion is organized around the assumption that androgyny is the state to which we all aspire (he says that "The woman's movement is merely the latest attempt to fulfill the objectives of orgasm"). His sexual bias is distracting, especially as he ignores women's struggles for political and legal rights, just as he overlooks a whole group of books by men who (in one way or another) openly took up the "Woman Question" in the eighties and nineties. Grant Allen, William Barry, Frank Frankfort Moore, George du Maurier, and Kipling represent the spectrum of male novelists' responses to the emotional challenge posed by feminist women, from the "high-mindedness" of the problem-novelist to the "brute virility" of male camaraderie in Rider Haggard's novels, to the male panic and fear expressed in du Maurier's *Trilby* and Kipling's *The Light that Failed*.[13] But if we can judge from these texts by male authors, Kiberd is fairly accurate in calling the most prevalent male responses to feminism "a defeatist self pity or an angry self assertion" (1985, 206). Specific manifestations of these feelings are sexual fantasy and potential violence.

Hardy and Gissing repeatedly expose men's tendencies toward violence or escapism in relation to women in their novels, and they do so with a broadness and a realism that makes them stand out from the works of their contemporaries—and with a nervousness, I should add, that distinguishes them from Meredith's more controlled treatment of similar themes. Their novels also stand out from those of their Victorian predecessors, for Hardy and Gissing write with a suggestive exactitude and explicitness that would have been inappropriate to mid-century audiences. There are scenes of masculine fantasy or violence in Dickens and George Eliot. Compare, for example, Hugh's attempted assault on Dolly Varden in *Barnaby Rudge* (a scene remarkably similar to Festus Derriman's attempted assault on Anne Garland in *The Trumpet-Major*), and Donnithorne's seduction of Hetty in *Adam Bede*, with Troy's sword exercise, the rape of Tess, and Lionel Tarrant's "courtship" of Nancy Lord in *In the Year of Jubilee*. All are scenes of attempted violence or sexual coercion.

The force of such scenes for mid-Victorian novelists was directed dialectically against the dehumanizing vices produced by society—their strength was in their capacity to uphold a moral code that was unchallenged and patriarchal. When Dickens, for example, describes Steerforth's seduction and abandonment of Em'ly in *David Copperfield*, he is conscientiously exploring a situation in which the tragedy—her "fall"—is brought about by a young man's rejection of a moral code that values self-control and fidelity, not to mention class integrity and the male duty to protect women. By the 1880s, feminist issues have made that code problematic, and the novels of Hardy and Gissing describe men and women fighting it out, with each other and with themselves, with little hope of a happy resolution. When Alec seduces Tess, the act is not described primarily as a crime committed against social morality as it is a challenge to society's definition of morality. Even the male protector, Angel Clare, is tragically too imbued with a patriarchal idea of feminine virtue to recognize a truly "pure woman." What is fascinating is that despite their feminism or their enlightened sexuality, male characters in Hardy and Gissing are nevertheless "completely subject to the psychological authority" of the patriarchal code (Harrison 1978, 4). Harvey Rolfe in *The Whirlpool*, for example, is a paragon of institutionalized masculinity and passive-aggressive egoism; but Gissing sympathizes with him as an open-minded, generous husband and conscientious father. And Hugh Carnaby in that novel is a real man's man who gives away his fear and insecurity at every turn. Their personalities, motives, desires—their masculine identity—is exposed within "the paradox of male privilege which the individual Victorian male would have felt both beneficial and restrictive."[14] This contradiction is central to masculine experience in late-century England.

Again, there is a wonderful passage in *The Way of All Flesh* that seems to capsulize the underside of male privilege and draw out its contradictions. The narrator, Mr. Overton, describes an incident from his boyhood:

> I remember when I was a boy myself I was once asked to take tea at a girls' school where one of my sisters was boarding. I was then about twelve years old. Everything went off well during tea-time, for the Lady Principal of the establishment was present. But there came a time when she went away and I was left alone with the girls. The moment the mistress's back was turned the head girl, who was about my own age, came up, pointed her finger at me, made a face and said solemnly, "A na-a-sty bo-o-y!" All the girls followed her in rotation making the same gesture and the same reproach upon my being a boy. It gave me a great scare. I believe I cried, and I know it was a long time before I could again face a girl without a strong desire to run away. (50–51)

The anecdote is interesting if viewed as a microcosm of adult society in Victorian England—the counterpart to the more secure male world of Eliot's Tom Tulliver or Dickens's Steerforth. The outwardly smooth and civilized relationship between the sexes, with its clearly defined roles of behavior and of social position, gives way to the male's subjective experience of being an alien in a feminized, domesticated space—of somehow polluting that space and yet being invited to participate in it. Sexual intimidation in this case provokes retreat (permanently, it seems—Overton never marries), and certainly Jude Fawley and Harvey Rolfe have "a strong desire to run away" from an impression of their latent "nasty" sensuality as well as from the disturbing presence of "new women." The girls' chanted sneer—"a na-a-sty bo-o-y!"—is as much a part of a man's masculine legacy as being "the man of the house" or the ruler of civilization. It is so much cultural and psychological baggage for many male characters in Hardy and Gissing, who seem to be struggling with an identity crisis as acute as women's in turn-of-the century England.

2
Nasty Boys: *The Emancipated* and *In the Year of Jubilee*

Male egoism is the subject of *The Emancipated* (1890) and *In the Year of Jubilee* (1894), but the object of these novels is not an exposé, such as Meredith intended in *The Egoist* (1879). In Gissing, male egoism is examined from the inside out, and the core is discovered to be not ignorance, but anxiety. Unlike Sir Willoughby's obtuse self-centeredness, Gissing's men are uncomfortably self-aware, partly because feminist issues make self-confrontation unavoidable. Gissing himself must have felt the contradictions inherent in the current definitions of masculinity, for his analyses of Lionel Tarrant, the young hero of *Jubilee*, and Reuben Elgar, the epitome of the modern male in *The Emancipated*, take on the nature of a dissection, or a peeling off of the various layers of attitudes that comprise masculinity, socially and even biologically. The process of Gissing's characterization is done from a clearly masculine point of view that is vacillating and inconsistent throughout, and therefore quite typical of late-nineteenth century experience.[1] It is a paradox of sexual stereotyping in Victorian society that women are imaged as indecisive, fickle, and contradictory, though the men who have created that image display the very faults they project on the social-sexual Other. John Goode explains that "Gissing's fictional structure demands . . . a plotless network of circumstance in which the possibilities of liberation are confined to mental states" and that women "are privileged by their very oppression to understand the psychology of that oppression and thus escape the vacillation it imposes on those who are mobile" (1978, 143). The psychological limitations inherent in men's social mobility brings to mind Hardy's paradoxical portrayals of female vacillation (Elfride, Eustacia, Bathsheba, Sue) and male steadfastness (Oak, Venn, Giles). There is a crucial difference, though, between male inconsistency in the two novels by Gissing and Hardy's capricious females: Tarrant and Elgar use their personal instability to maintain a stable social position of power and to justify their behavior to themselves and to women. In other words, unlike women, men want to keep their social/sexual role static. The peeling of layers of masculinity in these characters results in the reader's gradual understanding—and this is often lost to the character himself—that to be a man in his society is to be defined by imbalances. The novels pessimistically conclude without the genuine growth and enlightenment of male consciousness informed by men's experiences with women, feminists or not. Instead, Gissing shows a stubborn, almost masochistic adherence to patriarchal standards of male superiority and privilege. A socially reinforced self-centeredness blinds his characters to what they are doing to other people, but the narrator who has to tell the story is compelled to describe bad behavior, and we as readers see it as bad. The narrator's curious ambivalence is what keeps these novels from being feminist exposés of male egoism, but it is this very ambivalence that sharpens the novels into studies of the entrapped male psyche produced by the contradictions of Victorian masculinity.

"The brute instinct of male prerogative plied his brain to a frenzy." The line is from *The Emancipated* (418), and it can be used as the keynote of that book and of *Jubilee*. From the standpoint of masculine characterization, both are extremely tense psychological novels for Gissing's explorations of male characters delineates both "the brute instinct"—fierce sexual appetites—and "male prerogative"—socialized superiority over women. Contradictions are inherent in the interpretations of both these aspects of masculinity, which might be called private and public, and it is these contradictions that cause problems for Lionel Tarrant and Reuben Elgar.

In his excellent discussion of John Fowles's *The French Lieutenant's Woman* (1969), Bruce Woodcock explains how Victorian patriarchy reinforced anxiety over changing sexual codes by producing sexual categories for women, such as the madonna/magdalene syndrome, which created at the same time "a model of behavior against which men measured their own sexuality in ways as exacting as those expected of women" (1984, 83). Woodcock points to an important difference, however, between patriarchal imagery of women and that of men: whereas men required women to conform to sexual types in order to deprive them of social power, "the contradictions men forced themselves to live out were in the interests of maintaining their own social power as middle-class males" (1984, 83). The result was a personal anxiety about their public lives. Men felt the necessity of upholding institutions such as home and family that supported male power, but at the same time perceived a threat to that power that, I would argue, came as much from themselves as from feminists. Woodcock's emphasis on the anxiety created by the emergence of the New Woman is appropriate, but Gissing's novels are not just about male fear of female emancipation. Tarrant and Elgar embody a crisis in masculine identity in the last decades of the century that Fowles's protagonist, Charles Smithson, cannot fully represent as a man of the 1860s created by a man in the 1960s. And that is a crisis not only of social power— "male prerogative"—but of virility.

Gissing's men seem really goaded by sexual desire (in *The Whirlpool*, Harvey Rolfe wishes his infant son could remain in "the golden age" and avoid "manhood—the curse of sex developed"—328). Their sexual fantasies paradoxically consist of idealizing the woman they love as angel and moral redeemer, and despising her for her inferiority. Fear and resentment are expressed by abuse—physically, or by intimidation, desertion, or infidelity. Critics have discussed the psychological split represented by Alec d'Urberville and Angel Clare, which is a kind of recasting of the virgin/whore categories in male terms. In his biography, Michael Millgate links Hardy's fictional characterization with his intense personal relationship with Horace Moule, suggesting "the similarity between the names Angel and Alec opens up the further possibility that Hardy was deliberately dramatizing the two sides of Moule's fatally divided personality, its combination of extreme refinement with a capacity for sensual self-abandonment" (1982, 295). It is only a minor oversimplification to put the split in terms of the flesh/spirit dichotomy for the materialistic and spiritual impulses represent a central issue for Victorian novelists. G. J. Barker-Benfield, in *The Horrors of the Half-Known Life*, cites the primacy of men's habits of dividing themselves into mind and body, that "By definition they have been linked to man's beliefs about sex and the position of women, and his need to separate himself from and subordinate woman because she was the objective correlative of his own sexuality" (1976, xiii). In other words, by the 1880s, as Penny Boumelha explains, "the deadly war waged between flesh and spirit" to which Hardy refers in his Preface to *Jude* "had taken on a new significance . . . as the Darwinian notion of an extremely complex material world in constant change challenged the hitherto dominant form of the duality by reversing the priorities. The new dualism . . . makes the physiological organisation the determinant, with consciousness a kind of subsidiary product . . ." (1982, 138–39). The post-Darwinian emphasis on physiology, then, becomes a serviceable philosophy for virile late-Victorian men, who, after all, are only responding to natural and almost uncontrollable biological urges. There is no opportunity—or reason—to analyze motives and morals when a young man's "blood" is hot.

Gissing pays significant attention to body and intellect in his novels (and as I have suggested, *Tess* is centrally occupied with this antithesis); certainly for Tarrant and Elgar, the body is a kind of determinant, a controlling influence that causes them some anxiety partly because it seems so maddeningly, even violently, insurgent. Gissing's ordinary middle-class men use the same kind of blame-the-victim or blame biology rhetoric as Hardy's expert seducer, Alec d'Urberville, who at first coaxingly calls Tess "my Beauty" or "coz," but at the first show of resistance, curses her as a "young witch" and an "artful hussy." To Alec, "women's faces" are always to blame for male rapacity. After his conversion, he speaks to Tess as though she were responsible for rousing uncontrollable desires. He calls her "the innocent means of my backsliding" and "freakishly shaking her, as if she were a child," pleads "Why have you tempted me? I was firm as a man could be till I saw those eyes and that mouth again—surely there never was such a maddening mouth since Eve's! . . . You temptress, Tess; you dear damned witch of Babylon" (402). Alec accuses Tess of dragging him back to the flesh, to his sensuality, as Eve tempted Adam away from spiritual purity. Similarly, as I will discuss later in this chapter, Reuben Elgar reproaches his young wife, Cecily, for her failure to raise him up to an imagined level of feminine virtue in an incredible scene that exposes how sincere men are in their sophistry. Male justification for physical brutality or psychological manipulation of women seems to be the very fact of their maleness, as if there were something inherently bad about male sexual desire that takes over men's rational capabilities in ways women simply cannot understand as the objects (if instigators) of male passion. "What do you know," demands Elgar of his sister, Miriam Baske, "of a man whose passions boil in him like the fire on yonder mountain?" (62). One gets the impression that men are like guns ready to go off without warning, and their virility—a key word to "progressives" like

Grant Allen (who has one of his heroines declare that celibacy for a man "is impossible . . . cruel . . . wicked")[2]—is as much to be feared as to be protected.

In a new revisionist study of Hardy's heroines, Rosemarie Morgan says that there is "no equivalent among men of the madonna/whore polarisation" (1988, xii), and yet in *Tess* that bifurcation is quite clearly represented by the good Angel and the bad Alec. It is convenient to use Alec d'Urberville as a prototype of the tempted male, the demonic or Mr. Hyde half of the split male psyche. "I suppose I am a bad fellow—a damn bad fellow," he tells Tess. "I was born bad, I have lived bad, and I shall die bad in all probability" (125). His "badness" is the prodding masculine urge for self-satisfaction, power, and sexual dominance that has been institutionalized in Victorian patriarchal culture. In one sense, Alec's badness is part of the social construction of masculinity. Male chastity and fidelity may be middle-class virtues, but promiscuity and adultery make up middle-class reality. Gentlemen are not hard on themselves for living out these contradictions to the full. In *Far from the Madding Crowd*, Troy says, "Perhaps I am a bad man—the victim of my impulses" (179). There is a tinge of masculine pride beneath these confessions and self-accusations: a man may say he's a rogue or a scoundrel in his relationships with women, but by God, he's red-blooded. Masculine experience is virtually defined in Victorian society by just that—experience. "I have lived, and you know what that means in my language," says Elgar in *The Emancipated* (183). Indeed, it is hard to find a Victorian novel that does not include some tacit reference to how men "live." Even Angel Clare confesses to "eight-and-forty hours' dissipation with a stranger" in London (292), and, of course, Lydgate has his liaison with a Paris actress, and Rochester has his French mistress. The gentleman who intends to marry a woman of respectable family has most likely had his share of sexual experiences before the betrothal, and not necessarily with actresses and prostitutes.

Victorian society simply overlooked the exploitation of lower-class women by educated men. Steven Marcus makes a convincing case in suggesting that the author of *My Secret Life* may not be exaggerating his sexual adventures with maids, servants, and shop-girls (1964, 140–46). In a book about English education published in 1852, the American Charles Astor Bristed writes: "That shop-girls, work-women, domestic servants, and all females in similar positions, were expressly designed for the amusement of gentlemen, and generally serve that purpose, is a proposition assented to by a large proportion of Englishmen, even when they do not act upon the idea themselves."[3]

Victorian fiction concurs: Alec had "The Queen of Spades" before he had Tess (and at one point tells Tess, "yours was the worst case I ever was concerned in!"—393); Arthur Donnithorne seduces Hetty Sorrell in *Adam Bede*; Steerforth virtually abducts Em'ly; Barfoot in *The Odd Women* escapes entrapment by a village girl he seems to have exploited; Fitzpiers more than flirts with Suke Damson in *The Woodlanders*. There is a telling scene in chapter 7 of *In the Year of Jubilee*. Nancy Lord ditches her friends in the crowd so that she can independently explore the Jubilee celebrations, and not surprisingly she gets jostled by the mob, particularly by excited and unrestrained men. The first offender is a "young fellow of the clerkly order" who apologizes for stepping on her heel: "A push be'ind made me do it," he says (using an excuse, interestingly, that Hardy employs both metaphorically and literally in *Jude* and *Madding Crowd*).[4] The second incident is more sinister—"more noteworthy," according to the narrator—first, because it is a case of intentional assault, and second, because the man belongs to "some stratum of educated society" and Nancy, in her excitement, resembles "any shop-girl let loose." The basic information we can gather from this brief scene, as well as from the episodes mentioned above, is that despite Victorian standards of sexual restraint, chastity, and duty, novelists are able to describe how men of the upper ranks (even those with only a pretense to gentility, like Tarrant and Elgar) had an implicit sexual prerogative that they indulged not infrequently, and were in fact protective of, especially in the 1880s and 1890s with the growing asceticism of feminists who were more interested in suffrage than sex and in emancipation more than motherhood.

The impression that men felt their sexuality was being eclipsed by female aggression is reinforced in an essay published by Grant Allen in the *Fortnightly Review*, October 1889. "Now, we men are (rightly) jealous of our virility. We hold it a slight not to be borne that anyone should impugn our essential manhood. And we do well to be angry: for virility is the keynote to all that is best and most forcible in the masculine character."[5] But "virility" in 1889 has its underside. Tarrant and Elgar are outwardly persuaded of their virility, their attractiveness, and their power like Alec d'Urberville, Troy, Fitzpiers, Wildeve—all of Hardy's confident seducers. Inwardly, however, their egoistic self-assurance is steadily eroded by a perceived threat to their masculinity, which finally bursts into violence, anger, or especially in the case of Tarrant, rationalizations and flight. "The brute instinct of male prerogative"—virility, egoism, social privilege—is problematic for Gissing and Hardy in a way that is new to nineteenth-century fiction by male authors. It is not the villain in Gissing who is violent, self-centered, inconsistent, and cowardly, but the central protagonist, the psychological focus of the novel. Even Alec d'Urberville, admittedly the bad guy in *Tess*, cannot be too narrowly categorized as pure villain, simply because he is too self-aware. He suffers as much from his own baffled obsessions as he does from his crime against Tess. "I say in all earnestness that it is a shame for parents to bring up their girls in such dangerous ignorance of the gins and nets that the wicked may set for them," he says to her, with a suggestion that he is caught himself.[6] The contradictions that are built into the male protagonists in Gissing's novels—socially, in terms of the privilege of power and the anxiety over powerlessness, and sexually in the flesh/spirit struggle—are also built into the male novelist, which is why *The Emancipated* and *Jubilee* sometimes come across as excuses, explanations, and rationalizations of male egoism. There is less of this urgent sympathy for the male predicament in Hardy's novels. Many readers—understandably—become exasperated with Sue's manipulative vacillation, or disgusted by Bathsheba's folly and pride, but few commiserate with Jude or Oak primarily because they seem victimized either by these women, or by maddening sexual desire. This reaction can be explained partly because Hardy is able to sympathize with the essential human vulnerability of his female characters. Even Arabella Donn is not exactly villified for her survival strategies. Gissing's men, on the other hand, seem to be looking for sympathy and scapegoats— and, to some extent, are rewarded with both. But they are also seeking solutions to the extremes of violence and virtuousness they shift between in their sexual impulses.

The Emancipated, published a year before *Tess* in 1890, is a violent novel, and the central male psyche Gissing explores, twenty-seven-year-old Reuben Elgar, is distinguished by a tendency toward violence that is intellectualized into a virtue. His story is half of *The Emancipated*: one element of the plot concerns a young, pious, and severe widow, Miriam Baske, and her sexual and intellectual "emancipation" in the Bay of Naples, where she meets and falls in love with the English artist, Ross Mallard. The other strand in the plot deals with Miriam's brother,

Reuben Elgar, who joins her in Italy after a jaunt on the Continent
where he has been "improving himself." When he meets the
beautiful, unsullied Cecily Doran—Mallard's eighteen-year-old
ward—Elgar is smitten, and vows to become something of the
reformed rake for her love, but by the end of the novel, he has
managed to pull both himself and his virtuous wife into a scan-
dalous moral abyss.

Elgar is not a Michael Henchard, the passionate, tragic figure of
The Mayor of Casterbridge, who dies because of a combination of
character and circumstance. Elgar has rather a "muscular cowardliness," a stigma H. G. Wells and Morley Roberts attached to
Gissing himself.[7] He is really a type of the modern man, and he
proudly advertises himself as representative of his age. Gissing
seems intentionally to have created a character who exemplifies
the modern degenerate pseudo-intellectual. "It has taken me all
this time to outgrow the miserable misdirection of my boyhood,
and to become a man of my time. Thank the fates, I no longer live
in the Pentateuch, but at the latter end of the nineteenth century,"
says Reuben Elgar (66). Definitions of masculinity at "the latter
end of the nineteenth century" included qualities of vigor, intellectual precosity, passion, and ambition, and of course Grant
Allen's "keynote to all that is best and most forcible in the
masculine character"—virility. Despite his debaucheries and se-
ductions, Elgar's obsession, unlike Alec d'Uberville's, is not
women, but men, the nature of masculinity. He is really unable to
separate virility from violence, which is often self-directed. He is
also a consummate egoist. His conviction that his modern philosophy of life is correct and that his self-knowledge is complete
is so pathetically contradicted by his actions that it is hard to
believe that Gissing did not consciously take up as a theme of
this novel masculine self-delusion and self-destruction.

The modern philosophy that governs Elgar's behavior is a combination of determinism and what I would call moral dualism (by
which I do not necessarily mean the double standard, although
Elgar is convinced of its truth, as well). The flesh/spirit division
is taken to its extreme in Elgar's point of view so that his life's
activities can almost always fall into one of those two categories
and rarely overlap. He sometimes behaves (and justifies his behavior with creative irrationality) as though the mind is not
responsible for what the body is doing. "Because I was mad-
dened by sensual passion for a creature whom I never one moment respected, how did that lessen my love for you?" he asks his
wife. "Have I not told you a thousand times that in me soul and

body have lived separate lives?" (423). However separate, for
Elgar it is the body that is the determinant and that functions
outside of society's moral codes. Moreover, he is persuaded that
through the body, particularly through sensual adventures, he is
able to acquire a broader understanding of life, of modern
thought, and of himself. Supposedly it is his special self-
awareness and "literary" interest in social behavior that distinguish him from ordinary men—men such as the gentleman
lecher in the Jubilee crowd, or even "bad fellows" like Alec
d'Urberville. As a man, Elgar has been trained to nourish a
subjectivism that at its best may be self-understanding, and at its
worst is selfish egoism. His subjectivism is extreme and, I think,
grievously warped, but his impulse to make objects of what is the
sexual other is part of masculine ideology. Even Angel Clare is
disposed to view Tess with "a philosopher's regard of an exceedingly novel, fresh, and interesting specimen of womankind"
(186), and describes her as "actualized poetry" (225). In the same
way, Elgar uses a socialized male predisposition to objectify
female sexuality—Lydgate's "strictly scientific view of women"
(105)—in order to control and understand it; but Gissing shows
how this naming process deconstructs itself in Elgar's case, too,
for his "understanding" is as limited and self-centered as Angel's.
His agitation and restless mannerisms indicate that Elgar senses
and fears the weakness and insecurity beneath the virile image.
He is subject to "abrupt changes" when he speaks, is "never still"
but moves from chair to chair strumming his fingers, and he has a
nervous inclination to use a great deal of macho slang. When he
first appears in chapter 4, Elgar has a smile on his lips that
reveals "self esteem at odds with adversity," but what Gissing
subsequently describes in the novel is a man whose "self esteem"
is at issue with self ignorance and sexual anxiety.

In order to keep up his "self esteem" (a euphemism for his
threatened ego), Elgar needs to rationalize his years of profligacy
to his sister, Miriam, and he uses as his defense what patriarchal
Victorian society conveniently provides him, prerequisite male
experience. His amazing account of himself is worth citing fully,
because it makes up one of Elgar's central philosophical laws:

> "My life hitherto has not been wasted. . . . I have been gaining experi-
> ence. Do you understand? Few men at my age have seen more of
> life—the kind of life that is useful as literary material. It's only quite
> of late that I have begun to appreciate this, to see all the possibilities
> that are in myself. . . . All the disorder through which I have gone

was a struggle towards self-knowledge and understanding of my time. You and others are wildly in error in calling it dissipation, profligacy, recklessness, and so on. You, at least, Miriam, ought to have judged me more truly; you, at all events, should not have classed me with common men. . . . The nineteenth century is nothing to you; its special opportunities and demands and characteristics would revolt you if they were made clear to your intelligence. If I tell you I am before everything a man of my time, I suppose this seems only the cynical confession of all the weaknesses and crimes you have already attributed to me? It shall not always be so!" (66–67)

This speech exemplifies, on the one hand, the endurance of the doctrine of experience as making up the essential masculine character—something men use, by the way, to control women's lives too. (Elgar refuses Cecily her independence because she "hasn't enough experience to go on"—279.) It also reveals what may be the most important aspect of socialized male egoism: its sincerity. Gissing emphasizes not only Elgar's complete and earnest persuasion that he is not to be classed with "common men," but also other male characters' equal self-assurance and assumed self-knowledge. In Elgar's case, it is a pitiable and tragic delusion—the "special opportunities and demands" of nineteenth-century masculinity finally destroy him. But in the description of Clifford Marsh—a minor character in the British entourage in Naples, and a sort of watered-down Elgar—Gissing approaches Meredith-like satire:

He had a remarkable faculty of viewing himself in an ideal light, even whilst conscious that so many of his claims were mere pretense. Men such as Clifford Marsh do not say to themselves, "What a humbug I am!" When driven to face their conscience, it speaks to them rather in this way: "You are a fellow of fine qualities, altogether out of the common way of men. A pity that conditions do not allow you to be perfectly honest; but people in general are so foolish that you would get no credit for your superiority if you did not wear a little tinsel, practise a few harmless affectations. Some day your difficulties will be at an end, and then you can afford to show yourself in a simpler guise." (155)

For Marsh, "self-esteem had the force of irresistible argument" (154); the same can be applied to Elgar, but as a "man of his time" he is accomplished in other arguments, too, which help to justify his behavior.

Elgar's adherence to a deterministic creed exempts him from

responsibility and keeps his ego intact. Linked to the philosophical argument is a masculinist one that equates male sexuality
with the ungovernable forces of nature. The idea that his virility
is his destiny is confused in Elgar's mind with popular post-
Darwinian theories, and the conceptual mix turns out to be an
explosive one for Gissing's modern young man. Early in the
novel, Gissing demonstrates his awareness of how prevalent such
beliefs were in the minds of his contemporaries, and how sincerely they were adhered to. "What is all this nonsense about
weak men and strong men," says Elgar. "I act as I am bound to
act; I refrain as I am bound to refrain" (115). The narrator remarks: "This repeated expression of fatalism was genuine
enough. It manifested a habit of his thought. One of the characteristics of our time is that it produces men who are determinists
by instinct; who, anything but profound students or subtle rea-
soners, catch at the floating phrases of philosophy and recognize
them as an index of their being, adopt them thenceforth as
clarifiers of their vague self-consciousness" (115). "We are what
we are," Reuben tells his sister smugly (371), and to a considerable extent what he means is something like "boys will be boys."
Women supposedly are incapable of comprehending the primal
drives that govern male behavior; women do not feel the tor-
ments of love and desire, of sexual frustration, at the same pitch
as men; women, therefore, do not understand the urgency of
sexual consummation. A man's objectification of a woman is
partly due to his firm belief that the tortures of sexuality are a
private masculine experience, which accounts for the obstinacy
of Victorian men in love, who exhibit a stubborn persistence that
verges on coercion, even rape. Meredith's famous comic example
of the man who won't take no for an answer is Sir Willoughby
Patterne in *The Egoist,* but another of his characters, Nevil Beauchamp in *Beauchamp's Career* (1876), is not being funny when
he earnestly states that no matter what the woman says, "No case
is hopeless till a man consents to think it is" (63).

Reuben Elgar is a product of these patriarchal hypotheses (and
so is Gissing); they also emerge in other men in *The Emancipated,* even Ross Mallard, who is a sort of Rochester-Mr.
Knightley type. Mallard is so jealous of Elgar's relationship with
his "ward" Cecily that he feels it is a "disease clutching at his
vitals," which teaches him "fierceness, injustice, base suspicion,
brutal conjecture" (170). Mallard's half-protective, half-erotic love
for Cecily holds his imagination "with a terrible grip, burning,
torturing" (84). And indeed, even Elgar is so distracted by love

that he derives pleasure from driving the point of his pocketknife into his arm until the pain becomes intolerable (142).

That violence should be a part of a masculine ideology based partly on lawlessness and passion is not surprising, but it is important to remember that society requires the repression of rebellious tendencies. Elgar's emotionalism, his verbal aggression, is one manifestation of a masculine mystique, and perhaps of Gissing's own agitation during these years when he felt tortured by "sex-necessity" (Halperin 1982, 136). Elgar tries to explain himself to Miriam as though desire and temptation were alien experiences to women:

> What do you, with your nun's experiences, your heart chilled, your paltry view of the world through a chapel window, know of a man whose passions boil in him like the fire on yonder mountain? I should subdue my passions. Excellent text for a copy book in a girl's school! I should be another man than I am; I should remould myself; I should cool my brain with doctrine. With a bullet, if you like. (62)

This is a terrible harangue, but Gissing seems to intend it to be taken seriously. Men are victimized by these feelings, and men can be destroyed by them. "When I fume and rage like an idiot," says Elgar, "that's only the blood getting the better of the brain; an example of the fault that always wrecks me" (64).

Male "blood" is responsible for the wreckage of Elgar's life, and especially his disastrous relationship with Cecily Doran. Their courtship (if that is what it can be called) is defined by sexual urgency combined with distorted romanticism, evocative of the pressures adolescent boys place on girls to "go all the way." The divine lawlessness of love is a useful notion for excitable young men. "If a man falls in love, he thinks of nothing but how to gain his end," Elgar tells Mallard, and indeed his "blood" inspires him in some highly suspicious scenes of Victorian lovemaking. Elgar's virility verges on violence when Cecily reveals her reluctance to elope. "You must! I can't leave you! I had rather throw myself from these Capri rocks" (217). It is difficult to know if Gissing's hyperbolic language is intended to expose Elgar's immaturity and egoism, or show his macho-romantic desperation. Later in the scene, masculine strategies in lovemaking are effectively put down by feminine rationality. "Why does love make a man speak so bitterly and untruthfully? Nothing could make me do you such a wrong," says Cecily quietly. Elgar falls back on a deterministic version of biological necessity. Like Alec d'Urberville, he finds it convenient to blame female provocation and encouragement for male weakness, and demands remittance accordingly: "You have made me mad with love of you, and have no right to refuse to marry me when I show you the way!" (218) Here is the progressive young man exposing a latent mid-Victorian belief in patriarchal privilege.

But the role of the patriarch has built-in phobias: fear of failure and disenfranchisement. Inevitably, falling in love brings out the black side of Elgar's virility while exposing the blatant contradictions and inconsistencies in the masculine character, especially in "The Young Man of Promise" Gissing purposefully portrays in *The Emancipated* (141). Contemporary debate over the Woman Question included openly challenging sexual fallacies and stereotypes (the double standard, for example). Feminists also brought into the open the false and misleading mid-Victorian image of women as bearers of moral virtue and redeemers of male iniquity. Educated, up-to-date men of the time who professed to support women's rights would have rejected, at least ostensibly, the Victorian feminine ideal. In Reuben Elgar, Gissing portrays a modern man who is caught between the new images of women and the cherished old ones. "I am not going to talk rubbish about a woman's power to make a man angelic; that will do for third-rate novels and plays," he tells his sister (64), thereby demonstrating not only the spirit of the time, but also his own exalted realism. Of course, Elgar's actions are not compatible with his professed convictions, and at the end of the novel it is his confrontation with his own inconsistency that really causes his ruin.

Gissing seems straightforwardly critical in his descriptions of Elgar's modern ideas, his self-centered inactivity, and philosophical ignorance, but if there is a sense of the author's ambivalence toward his male characters in *The Emancipated*, it emerges in the scenes between Reuben and Cecily, where a man's self-image is gradually eroded by an obtrusive reality. In one of the first altercations with Cecily after their marriage, Elgar doggedly makes his case against her in a "half-embarrassed way" (256)—a revealing narrative aside, for Elgar's dissatisfaction is with himself, not with his wife, and he vaguely understands this. He views Cecily's clear-sightedness and common sense as dangerously subversive, threatening not only to strip him of his domestic power over her, but also to expose his sense of personal instability. She tells him, "You have become an idealist of a curious kind; you like to think of me as an emancipated woman, and yet, when I have the opportunity of making my independence practical, you show

yourself alarmed. I am not sure that I understand you entirely"
(278). The female perspective on male behavior is seldom described in novels by men in terms of such blank confusion.
Cecily's judgment is a clue to Gissing's real sensitivity to
women's positions, reminiscent of Grace's thought, in *The Woodlanders*, that "Men were so strange" (352), or of Clara Middleton's
exasperation in *The Egoist*—"Oh, men! men! They astounded the
girl; she could not define them to her understanding. Their
motives, their tastes, their vanity, their tyranny, and the domino
on their vanity, the boldness of their tyranny, clenched her in
feminine antagonism to brute power" (273). All three women are
interested more in saving themselves than in saving men, and yet
Gissing seems to think that Reuben Elgar is in need of salvation.
The picture of Elgar in the last two-thirds of the novel is that of a
man whose unwilling descent into his own consciousness resembles a willful descent into a self-created hell. Here Gissing
describes male confusion and desperation as patriarchal assumptions of superiority and sexual potency begin to break
down.

Elgar does not understand his behavior or see his position
clearly, but the narrator does: "Disguise it how he might, he was
simply in the position of a husband who fears that his authority
over his wife was weakening. . . . The more he felt his inconsistency, the more arbitrary he was compelled to be. Motives confused themselves and harassed him. In his present mood, the
danger of such a state of things was greater than he knew" (298).
The "danger" alluded to is sexual adventurism—first a two-day
affair with a shop-girl, then desertion and profligacy of a more
generalized sort. When he returns home, the ensuing scene epito-
mizes the contradictory forces at work in the masculine psyche:
self-pity and defiance, self-love and self-hatred, virility and impotence. His impassioned speech exposes how absolutely Elgar
clings to mid-Victorian notions of women, and how sincerely he
believes his actions are vindicated by sexual urges out of his
control:

> "I looked up to you as a high-minded woman, and I loved you for
> your superiority to myself. . . . Because I was maddened by sensual
> passion for a creature I never one moment respected, how did that
> lessen my love for you? You complain that I kept away from you; I did
> so because I was still racked by that vile torment, and shrank in
> reverance from approaching you. You might have known me well
> enough to understand this. Have I not told you a thousand times that
> in me soul and body have lived separate lives? Even when I seemed

sunk in the lowest depths, I still loved you purely and truly; I loved you all the more because I was conscious of my brutal faults. Now you have destroyed my ideal; you have degraded yourself in my esteem . . . I can never forgive you." (423)

Elgar fears he will sink "down and down, lower and lower into the bestial life" unless Cecily redeems him—"implore her to save me, only out of pity," he begs Miriam (451–52). His pitiful weakness and child-like supplications are the counterparts to self-loathing, violence, and misogyny (he is "devilishly tempted" to strike Miriam across the face with a stick in chapter 17). Elgar confesses to feeling "murderous impulses" toward both his sister and Cecily, but the impulses are finally self-directed. The women survive; the "man of his time" ends up being shot in the head by the husband of a Parisian actress.

By relating Elgar's death secondhand (stumbled across in a French newspaper with the paragraph about "en jeune Anglais" circled), Gissing may be trying to insert a male-oriented moral to a cautionary tale: the cult of virility must be tempered with Actonian self-control and forbearance. But the narrator's final reluctance to objectify the male experience (less unusual when male novelists focus on women) lends a muted sympathy to Elgar's position. Gissing would seem to support sociologist Andrew Tolson's thesis that "'masculinity' is structured in ambivalence" (1977, 24) as much in his own voice in The Emancipated as in his male characterization for if the novel is open to a masculinist interpretation that socialized male egoism and undisciplined "virility" are destructive parts of Victorian masculinity, it, at the same time, leaves us with the impression that Gissing would rather evade the issue. He seems to suggest that there is something forgiveable if not admirable about Elgar for being so impulsive for he proves he is alive, and considering the prevailing atmosphere of inertia toward the end of the century, that is something. Elgar is "man enough," so to speak, to be driven and swayed by Conrad's "strong, lusty, red-eyed devils" instead of the flabby ones. This is a quality of which Gissing, as a man, tacitly approves.

Grant Allen's authoritative definition of what it means to be a man in his novel The Woman Who Did, published in 1895, throws considerable light on the ambivalence Gissing projects in his treatment of masculine character as an insider:

The right sort of man doesn't argue with himself at all on these matters. He doesn't say with selfish coldness, "I can't afford a wife";

or "If I marry now, I shall ruin my prospects." He feels and acts. He mates like the birds, because he can't help himself. A woman crosses his path who is to him indispensible, a part of himself, the needful complement of his own personality, and without heed or hesitation, he takes her to himself, lawfully or unlawfully, because he has need of her. (25)

The same attitude is echoed by forty-two-year-old Edmund Langley in Gissing's *Sleeping Fires*, also published in 1895: "[G]ive yourself to the man whose supreme need is the need of you," he argues passionately. "Yield yourself to a man's love, and be perfect woman" (95). This is the ideological base Gissing's characters live within as men in 1895. It is a principle of sex and love that his characters follow quite confidently, and in the same spirit as a Sir Willoughby who can declare, "For when I love, I love. . . . There can be no medium, not with me" (262). Elgar's egoism and reckless virility, and his pathetic dependence on the very women he calls his inferiors is evocative of D. H. Lawrence's attitude toward this kind of needy machismo—Gudrun's bitterness in *Women in Love* (1920) toward "the Arthur Donnithornes, the Geralds of the world. So manly by day, yet all the while such a crying of infants in the night" (458). Possibly, Elgar represents an extension of Gissing's own anxieties under the current definitions of masculinity—he is portraying "the right kind of man" who "feels and acts," yet we are left with an impression that Elgar is a very wrong kind of man indeed, a d'Urbervillesque "bad fellow" who is trapped and destroyed, not by women, but by himself.

In the Year of Jubilee (1894) is another three-decker with intertwining plots, but the focus is most often upon the relationship between Lionel Tarrant, a rather ordinary pseudo-genteel young man, and Nancy Lord, an even more ordinary bourgeois young woman, who is psychologically pulled between her desires for independence and for love. She "wins" Tarrant, who seduces her and is forced to marry her when she reveals that she is pregnant. Nancy never really secures Tarrant's love, as he flees all material responsibility after their clandestine marriage, and ultimately creates an arrangement where he can live out the masculine version of conjugal bliss in a separate flat from his wife. In this novel, the egoist triumphs, at least materially. Spiritually, though, Lionel Tarrant is still a victim of his sexuality, as are virtually all the male characters in *Jubilee*, who at some point feel racked by sexual desire. The violent language used to describe sexual arousal is reminiscent of Elgar's outbursts and threats, and is informed with the kind of uncontrollable virility that defined "the right sort of man" in the 1890s. Rhetorically, at least, Gissing associates sensual appetites with tormenting biological necessity. Luckworth Crewe, Nancy's first suitor, with "lips parted hungrily" follows her "warm cheek and full lips"; her brother, Horace Lord—by far the most crudely sensual male character—"burned and panted" at the proximity of a woman's "white flesh"; and Tarrant of course exculpates his seduction/abduction of Nancy Lord because he was "goaded by his raging blood" (104; 89; 180).

Male sexuality is linked to a natural predatoriness, which is one half of Grant Allen's "prime antithesis—the male, active and aggressive; the female, sedentary, passive, and receptive" (1908, 78). Gissing's novel articulates the modern urge to find a biological origin for sex roles, the basis for Havelock Ellis's massive scientific treatise, *Men and Women*, published the same year as *Jubilee*. Notably, it is a male preoccupation, intent on enforcing the double standard and making aggressive and independent women appear unnatural viragos. Gissing reveals his anxieties about "unnatural" women in his portrayal of the frigid intellectual, Jessica Morgan, and of the bitchy, unmaternal Peachey women. He also betrays his ambivalence toward "natural" men by exploring the Victorian code of middle-class respectability from the standpoint of a hot-blooded (if sexually confused) protagonist, Lionel Tarrant, whose egoism rivals that of Reuben Elgar.

The narrator's attitude in this novel, however, is problematic not because of its ambivalence, but because of its obedience to the social and sexual prejudices the book pretends to challenge. For example, the ideology of "Nature" has serious implications for women, so serious that when Nancy Lord calmly and philosophically explains that you can put up with a great deal if you feel you're following a law of Nature, we get the impression that Gissing is indulging in some wish-fulfillment about female acquiescence. We can almost sense some authorial discomfort in women's resolute speeches: "Now, I have brains, and I should like to use them; but Nature says that's not so important as bringing up the little child to whom I have given life. One thought that troubles me is, that every generation of women is sacrificed to the generation that follows; and of course that's why women are inferior to men" (404–5).

Lloyd Fernando sees Nancy Lord as evidence of Gissing's "con-

tinual efforts to understand the new role women sought to play
in society" (1977, 120–21), but obviously it is not Nancy who is
seeking a "new role." Tarrant is more oppressed by conventional
sex roles than the women in this novel, and he is actively seeking
a utopian quasi-bachelorhood that would permit the piquancy of
having a mistress without the boredom and claustrophobia of
putting up with a wife. Fernando goes on to say that in Gissing's
novels and in *Jubilee* in particular, "men are absolved from any
significant revaluation of their own role" (1977, 121). This is
partially true, and in fact consistent with the masculine emphasis on action over contemplation. But *Jubilee* is full of implicit
revaluations of male roles simply because the novel is centrally
concerned with sexual relationships, and men are not spared a
good long look in the mirror. Self-confrontation for Lionel Tarrant comes like a jolt after his "mere seduction" of Nancy Lord
(361) when his role changes from lover to husband to father with
bewildering speed. "Significant revaluation" does not mean, necessarily, accurate and enlightening self-analysis. In Gissing, it
may also mean creative irrationality, and I would say that Tarrant
excels in introspections of this sort. And he survives, literally,
though it is a shabby and cowardly survival. One could argue
along with John Halperin that the narrator's gratuitous attacks on
women and Tarrant's self-righteous tone reflect Gissing's growing
animosity toward his wife (1982, 198–207). The Peachey marriage is, indeed, the proper focus for a biographical reading of the
book. In the character of Tarrant, though, *In the Year of Jubilee*
resembles *Born in Exile* as a study of "the falsifying processes of
desire" for men (Poole, 1975, 199), and how "liberal-minded"
male characters seem to prefer the falsification even after the
desire has been satisfied.

Tarrant's sexuality is not like Reuben Elgar's—not as explosive
or savage, or as temperamentally built-in to his character. If Elgar
is nervous and hyperactive, Tarrant is possessed by "a chronic
languor" (51), which is nonetheless not to be mistaken for
effeminacy. Tarrant is not a "fop or a weakling," not "emasculate": "his movements merely disguised the natural vigour of a
manly frame," and he is physically attractive to women (51).
Even his "conceit . . . was in the main amiable" (51). Though he
is not on the verge of sexual eruption, Tarrant is a man who, like
Alec, Troy, Wildeve, and Fitzpiers, is "looking about him"—more
particularly, below him, at women of a lower class—for flirtatious
if not promiscuous affairs. He watches Nancy Lord with "condescending gratification"—an example of the proprietary air upper-

class men assume in regarding women—and she feels "a conviction that he had often bestowed this look upon girls of a class below his own" (114). Unfortunately for Tarrant, Nancy's rank is not low enough (her father was a well-to-do piano salesman) and his casual amour with her wrecks his life when he is compelled to act honorably and marry her. The narrator (perhaps not surprisingly) sympathizes with the male predicament and supplies his character with a solution: by living apart from Nancy, Tarrant is rewarded with both a mistress and a wife. This solution smacks of the masculine anxiety to keep separate the sexual categories of madonna and magdalen, and by association their male counterparts, Alec/Angel, seducer and husband. Despite Gissing's fantasizing tendency in this novel, the troublesome dichotomy between flesh and spirit, translated into a pseudo-genteel Victorian mentality, emerges as the central problem for Lionel Tarrant: the difference between "a moral attachment" and "a passionate desire" (193).

Desire is mystifying for Tarrant, and so he blames women for tempting him, but sexual attraction is just as frightening and enigmatic for Nancy. Because she feels superior to Luckworth Crewe, he neither intimidates nor arouses her. Tarrant, however, makes her feel "a soft and deliberate subdual of the will to dreamy luxury" that engenders "a sense of peril" (115; 118). She is right to feel alarmed, for Tarrant is hardly in control of his "raging blood." He seems at first only interested in indulging in erotic play with her, very similar to Alec's pleasure in feeding Tess strawberries or teaching her to whistle—with some of the same threatening overtones. The subtleties of his flirtation are not original, nor are they very sincere, and Gissing gives a probably accurate picture of genteel Victorian lovemaking, complete with romantic platitudes, flattery, and socialized concepts of male passion that have shifted from repression to aggression. Tarrant is playing a role: "Look at me again like that—with the eyes half-closed, and the lips half-mocking," he says rapturously. "Oh the exquisite lips! If I might—if I might. . . . Let me look at you for a few minutes more!" (126). He aestheticizes her out of existence. There is a sense of terrible phoniness and affectation in Tarrant's desire, the impression that the scene has been rehearsed too many times. It is quite different from d'Urberville's fascination with Tess, which seems strikingly genuine in comparison, even despite his self-declared profligacy. Gissing's "bad fellow" advertises himself as a product of his day, and all the fundamental socialized principles of masculinity—egoism, social privilege,

sexual urgency, misogyny disguised as chivalry—are revealed in
his commonplace lovemaking that has an all too common result:
her pregnancy. When he crowns her with ivy, when he recites
Keats and the "old poet" who "talked of bees seeking honey on
his lady's lips" (131), when he touches her waist, kisses her
lightly, grabs her hands because he is "conquered," Tarrant is
applying all the stock techniques idle young men use to gain
sexual favors—men such as those in "the Hodiernals," his infor-
mal London club. David Pugh, in his study of nineteenth-century
American men, *Sons of Liberty*, uses Tocqueville's distinction
that " 'in the United States men seldom compliment women, but
they daily show how much they esteem them,' a trait he felt was
opposite to the European male's excessive use of flattery as a
means of expressing his contempt for women" (55). Tarrant later
proves the point, and unconsciously condemns his own behavior
when he criticizes the "maudlin humbug" men say to women to
"disguise that truth" of male superiority to women in force of
mind and body (414).

Tarrant's shallow typicality is the real indictment of Victorian
masculinity, the self-satisfaction that resembles Reuben Elgar's
pride at representing the nineteenth-century male. Tarrant is a
self-described "up-to-date" gentleman, "critical of Today, ap-
prehensive of Tomorrow" (144); and like modern men, he con-
templates the female sex as object/other, placing women in strict
categories. "His view of woman—the Hodiernals talked much of
woman—differed considerably from his thoughts of the individual woman with whom he associated; protesting oriental sympathies, he nourished in truth the chivalry appropriate to his years
and to his education, and imagined an ideal of female excellence
whereof the prime features were moral and intellectual" (144).
"Female excellence" for Tarrant is inextricably linked to class, as
well, and he is quick to blame Nancy for having only a "charlatan
'education' " whose "cheap philosophies" fail to teach women to
"protect" themselves (141). Women like Nancy are a "social
peril" for young men.

Gissing seems to suggest that to be sexually active is like
walking through a mine field, even leaving aside fears about
venereal disease.[8] Middle-class lovemaking for men has moral as
well as financial implications when it takes place outside of the
brothels. The threat of entrapment is as intimidating as public
accusations of blackguardism. Tarrant thinks women (and authorial agreement is implied) should play by the rules, but he
does not perceive that the sexes may be operating from two
separate standards, which Tarrant manipulates to his advantage

when convenient. Marital fidelity is as conditional for Tarrant as it was for Elgar. "Faithful in the technical sense, he had not been, but the casual amours of a young man caused him no self reproach" (338). Men know that there are two kinds of women in the world, but as Tarrant reviews his situation, he is forced to face the fact that he approached Nancy as one kind—sexually available and socially inferior—and ended by finding he had placed her in the wrong category. After the elliptical episode in part III, chapter 6, where he "carries her through the brushwood, away into the shadow of the trees" (133), the playful flirtation turns into serious courtship, to Tarrant's naive surprise:

> But as for marriage, he would as soon have contemplated taking to wife a barmaid. Between Miss Lord and the young lady who dispenses refreshment there were distinctions, doubtless, but none of the first importance. Then arose the question, in what spirit, with what purpose, did he seek her intimacy? The answer he simply postponed.
>
> And postponed it very late indeed. Until the choice was no longer between making love in idleness, and conscientiously holding aloof; but between acting like a frank blackguard, and making the amends of an honest man. (146)

Tarrant's story, so far, seems to be a cautionary tale for men, and the moral is to be familiar with your motives before you get familiar with a woman. But Gissing is too sympathetic to men's awkward situation in respectable society to simply blame Tarrant for his lack of understanding. There is a suggestion of the socially and historically reinforced male view of women as sexual "conquests"—Gissing applies the very word—who, if they do not expressly protest, are understood to implicitly permit sexual advances. "The girl's fault, to be sure," thinks Tarrant.

> Love, in that sense of the word which Tarrant respected, could not be said to influence him. He had uttered the word; yes, of course he had uttered it, as a man will who is goaded by his raging blood. But he was as far as ever from loving Nancy Lord. Her beauty . . . had lured him on; his habitual idleness, and the vagueness of his principles, made him guilty at last of what a moralist would call very deliberate rascality. He himself was inclined to see his behavior in that light; yet why had Nancy so smoothed the path of temptation? (147)

Because Nancy did not "exercise the common prudence of womanhood" (148), Tarrant is compelled to "act honorably" and probably spoil his life (149). Gissing is clearly persuaded of the

idea that women need to be sexually vigilant to keep uncontrollable male sexual instincts in check. Both women and men in the
novel affirm that a man's philandering and aggressiveness are
"natural," and that a "worthy woman" would keep him out of
danger. Sexually susceptible Horace Lord, unfortunate enough to
be in love with sensual, vulgar Fanny French, is doomed to
corruption, "For it was the result of this girl's worthlessness that
Horace . . . had come to regard women with unconscious cynicism. He did not think he could be loved for his own sake, but he
believed that, at any time, the show of love . . . might be won by
display of cash" (237). Crewe matter-of-factly states that "A man
can't trust himself about women till he's thirty or near it" (103).
The most effective statement of Gissing's belief in the essential
salaciousness of male nature comes resignedly from Nancy. "You
behaved as most men would," she tells her husband, who winces
under the reproach mainly because it classifies him with common men. "He would much rather have been accused of abnormal villainy" (374).

Gissing's efforts to vindicate Tarrant on the grounds of masculine "nature" and feminine weakness obviously differ from,
for instance, Hardy's picture of Jude as Arabella's innocent victim. Nancy is less sensual and aggressive, more self-deprecating,
and marriage through entrapment is the farthest thing from her
mind. Nevertheless, Tarrant does feel trapped materially and
psychologically by Nancy's sexuality, and his instinct for self-
preservation, his constitutional egoism, makes it impossible for
him to empathize with her situation. Whereas she is anxious
about his fidelity, he is wondering if she is "a domestic person"
(154). Her guilt at concealing the marriage from her father and her
fear of pregnancy are countered by Tarrant's genteel disinclina-
tion to face "the chilling prospect" of having to work to support a
family (199). All of Tarrant's speeches about "the whole duty of a
wife who wishes to be loved," the Godwinian proposal of living
apart, and the declarations of male responsibility to "join in the
rough-and-tumble" (429) are a confused melange of the most
dominant sexual attitudes of the day. The old sexual prohibitions, which have broken down by the 1890s, are being replaced
by radical notions of sex and marriage (often mistakenly identified as feminist) that Gissing uses to justify Tarrant's actions. But
the reactionary strain dominates the ostensible liberalism of his
words: Tarrant is, in fact, appalled by his involvement with
Nancy because he is forced to admit that she has claims upon
him. When she alludes to the possibility of pregnancy, his emo-

tional response is disbelief followed by repulsion. "This indeed had not entered into his calculations. . . . And now he arraigned mother-nature, the very divinity whom hitherto he had called upon to justify him. All at once he grew cold to Nancy . . . abhorred the change that must come over Nancy herself. Nancy a mother—he repelled the image, as though it degraded her" (180). He fears for his liberty and is disgusted physically by Nancy's maternity. The sexual freedom he indulged has thus turned into bondage, and the beautiful female ideal into sordid animality. Tarrant's flight to the West Indies (like Angel Clare's in the same direction) is outwardly rationalized as a necessary business venture, but inwardly Tarrant is panting "to escape from her" (201). Nancy's female reality had intruded upon Tarrant's male fantasy; he seeks to escape a conventional marriage that would transform his sexually provocative mistress into a sexually functional wife. Tarrant's psychological inconsistency is shared by the d'Urberville side of masculine identity, but essentially turned around. Alec wants to "act honourably" by making his mistress his wife, whereas Tarrant wants to make his wife into a mistress. Indeed, his impulse to be magnanimous and noble is greater when he imagines himself in the role of a gallant, not a husband, just as Alec is moved to aid Tess after he has most injured her. Tarrant feels, "without this legal bondage, it would have been much easier to play a manly part at the time of Nancy's becoming a mother. Were she frankly his mistress, he would not be keeping thus far away when most she needed the consolation of his presence" (339).

It is significant that these men are most capable of feeling "the glow of virtue" (205) after they have gotten what they want from women, and feel luxuriously penitent. "Female defencelessness is precious to the male's sense of sexual vanity; his belief in his own potency is enhanced by the sight of a woman who has been denied the means of resistance," Fraser Harrison explains in *The Dark Angel* (1978, 28). Elgar's pathetic pleas for salvation after his abusive behavior toward Cecily reflect a sensibility similar to Troy's excessive grief over Fanny *(Far from the Madding Crowd)*, or Fitzpiers's remorse over his infidelity *(The Woodlanders)*. It is effectively a chivalric worship of women conducted from a position of strength, and designed to reinforce that position. Harrison goes on to say that by "attributing to women the possession of certain saintly virtues, men ensured that in the process women were prevented from exercising their more practical capabilities and from indulging their earthlier emotions" (115)—such as

Cecily's social independence in *The Emancipated* and Nancy's novel-writing, shop-work, and motherhood.

By the 1890s, the male position had been perceptibly weakened since troublesome, independent-minded wives are even a subject of mainstream novels. Men tried to "shore up and conserve their privileges" (Harrison 1978, 116) from the coming revolution by persistently adhering to myths of female inferiority, dependence, and sexual innocence. Tarrant leaves his pregnant wife for an indefinite time to "work for your future," and assures her "to protect you is my duty and I shall not fail it" (204, 205). His magnanimity rests firmly on a contradictory masculine ethos, something Gissing surely understood, in which men are privileged to bend the moral code—the value of Experience, the "natural" forcefulness of sex—but are still inescapably governed by it, at least in the middle classes. When the double standard backfires, Tarrant really feels he has no choice: the code of male honor says he must marry Nancy, and the code of male permissiveness forbids him to be bound to her. He rationalizes his desertion in the most self-flattering terms: he is going away, unselfishly, to serve her best interests. Alec d'Urberville eventually acts on the same principle. Ironically, he wants to "save" Tess from her husband's desertion—"I know what men are," he tells her (438). Both Hardy and Gissing, it seems, are subtly keyed into the willing self-deception of "bad fellows" and moral cowards. They also expose the tenacity of mid-Victorian values of chivalric manliness, layered beneath a cult of self-protective virility and fear of powerlessness.

In late-century novels, then, the opposite side of Sir Charles Grandison's gentlemanliness, Dobbin's patient devotion, or Mr. Harding's moral decency is not a fictional villain or an opponent to the protagonist. It is something within the protagonist himself. The narrator of *The French Lieutenant's Woman* calls *Dr. Jekyll and Mr. Hyde,* published in 1886, "the best guidebook to the age" (319).[9] Similarly, the Alec/Angel model of masculine identity is vital to any interpretation of Victorian masculinity—especially in that for Hardy, the martyr is also a madman, as I will discuss in the next chapter. D'Urberville and Reuben Elgar recognize their badness as something built into their masculinity, a deterministic downward-spiraling sexual affliction, and though not forgiveable (the imagery that surrounds Alec, for example, is certainly intentionally diabolic), it is not completely censurable to the male novelist, who is himself adjusting to a changing male ethic.

Lionel Tarrant's cowardliness and conceit cannot be vindicated on account of his manliness, which Gissing seems inclined to demonstrate. Partly this is because the character has no feminine enemy—he is not fighting for dear life with a bitchy Ada Peachey or a vulgar Fanny French. But at the same time, he is not sharply contrasted with a virtuous woman such as Cecily in *The Emancipated*, or Tess. After all, as Adrian Poole points out, Nancy Lord is "not specially gifted" (1975, 197). Poole is correct to say, though, that her ordinariness is part of the novel's strength, for Tarrant's pseudo-radical speeches about the brutality of "hugger-mugger marriage," and his outrageously sexist generalizations ("there is not one wife in fifty thousand who retains her husband's love after the first year of marriage"—410) are pitifully lost on the young woman who is seduced, clandestinely married, pregnant, deserted, and forced to work.

"[G]iven Tarrant's consistent failure in the course of the novel to engender any emotion in the reader other than that of repulsion," says Poole, "we cannot feel that his demand for a new sort of star-like polarity is anything much more than male egoism trying to escape the responsibilities of a truly mutual relationship" (1975, 197). The critic's implicit reference to Birkin's ideal in *Women in Love* is notable, and in a sense Tarrant's irksome speeches are anxious, ill-considered versions of the Lawrentian doctrine of sexual polarity.[10] But in the modern state of "sexual anarchy" (letter to Bertz, 2 June 1893, p. 171) emotional and sexual fulfillment is virtually impossible. The men in *Born in Exile*, *Eve's Ransom*, *New Grub Street*, and *The Whirlpool*, all end up without sexual partners, for better or for worse. Even Henry Ryecroft says in his *Private Papers*,

> Yes, but is there any mortal in the whole world upon whom I could invariably depend for sympathetic understanding?—nay, who would even generally be at one with me in appreciation? Such harmony of intelligence is the rarest thing. All through life we long for it: the desire drives us, like a demon, into waste places; too often ends by plunging us into mud and morass. And, after all, we learn that the vision was illusory. To every man it is decreed: Thou shalt live alone. (57)

These sentiments partly reflect Gissing's feeling of personal exile, which he suffered throughout his career. They also invoke the modern urge toward a separation of one's inner self from an outside world, which is perceived as uncomfortably feminine.

Sexuality—men's "blood," the "sex-necessity"—still remains problematic. If one way for male characters to keep the problem of sexual desire under control is to blame biology or women—to, in effect, elevate male promiscuity to the status of healthy virility—then another way is to suppress or ignore sexual urges altogether. In chapter 3, I will explore how Hardy treats the opposite side of the virility code, that is, the chivalric or gentlemanly ideal of male behavior. Though the reverse of Gissing's masculine models, Hardy's repressed men in *Far from the Madding Crowd* and *The Woodlanders* exemplify the same anxieties as Elgar and Tarrant. Both authors suggest that if withdrawal from women, the threatening Other, seems initially possible to late-century men, retreat from themselves and their own sexuality is not.

3

Pathological Gentlemen: *Far from the Madding Crowd* and *The Woodlanders*

In *Far from the Madding Crowd* (1874), Matthew Moon contributes philosophically to the rustics' gossip about Bathsheba and Troy by saying, " 'Twas only wildness that made him a soldier, and maids rather like your man of sin" (174). Certainly the women in Hardy's and Gissing's novels frequently fall for the unscrupulous seducer, and sometimes boldness is more attractive to women than reliability. Miss Aldclyffe in *Desperate Remedies* (1871) says quite frankly, "The love of an inconstant man is ten times more ardent than that of a faithful man—that is, while it lasts" (97). And in *A Pair of Blue Eyes* (1873), we are told that the heroine, Elfride Swancourt, "had her sex's love of sheer force in a man, however ill-directed" (179).

Hardy's doomed, amorous couples—Bathsheba and Troy, Grace and Fitzpiers, Eustacia and Wildeve—are counterparts to the shabby urbanites Gissing pairs in *The Emancipated* and *In the Year of Jubilee*. The "man of sin" is attractive, passionate, sexually experienced, and prone to infatuation. Indeed, his is "the love of men like Fitzpiers [which] is unquestionably of such quality as to bear divisions and transference" (266). If male aggression and sexual promiscuity seem built into these men's habits and constitutions, passivity and chastity are as addictively appropriated by their saintly male opposites. "The neurotic voyeur" and "the impotent spectator" are Albert Guerard's names for the passive heroes in Hardy's novels, men such as Gabriel Oak, Winterborne, Diggory Venn, Clym Yeobright, and to a lesser extent, Angel, Henry Knight, and Jocelyn Pierston.[1] The lack of normal aggressiveness in these men, Guerard explains, "suggests an area of abnormal feeling dramatized without awareness of its abnormality—the unconscious study of a neurosis, perhaps unconscious biography" (1949, 114). It is this unconscious and almost pathological passivity that is the reverse extreme of the

cult of masculine virility and aggression. The Victorian code of
Christian manliness is largely the basis for such unaggressive
and, above all, patient super-gentlemen in Hardy, and it is a
doctrine the male author approves of with typical ambivalence.
As Guerard puts it, "Hardy constructed an ethic of fidelity and
generous simplicity, but not an ethic of rejection. He identified
himself to a degree with his sexless and self-denying heroes and
so could not withhold imaginative sympathy. But he also crit-
icized their habits of renunciation, their immature refusal to
accept life and enjoy it" (1949, 119).

The ethic of forbearance and scrupulousness seems the polar
opposite of Gissing's or Grant Allen's ethic of virility and passionate surrender to "nature," another example of the Alec/Angel
psychological division. But despite their "reserve and restraint"
(Giles Winterborne's virtues), Hardy's less stereotypically virile
heroes exhibit similar tendencies toward self-destruction, chan-
nelled into heroic self-sacrifice for the sake of an idealized
woman. There is a great deal of will and energy in Boldwood and
Giles Winterborne, the two characters I will focus upon in this
chapter, but it is (to be oxymoronic) energy grossly refined. These
men lack sexual experience and so their obsessions are of a
different kind—not sensual, but spiritual. They are, in fact, the
perverse embodiments of what the "bad fellows" temporarily
revert to in their remorseful moods. Indeed, Fitzpiers "almost
envied Giles his chivalrous character" (402). Masculine valor is
prized even by those men incapable of exhibiting it, while, ironically, it destroys those who do.

Chivalry is conspicuous in Winterborne, and overall it is a
moral code that, however much romanticized, was exceedingly
important in the nineteenth century, especially after 1850.
Linked to chivalry, of course, is the notion of "muscular Chris-
tianity"; Thomas Hughes gave a crucial explication of the term in
Tom Brown at Oxford (1861), declaring that "the crown of all real
manliness, of all Christian manliness, is purity."[2] He does not
mean celibacy, but rather the sexual act accompanied only by
faithful affection and, at mid-century, sacred matrimony (by
1895, Grant Allen could assert that "Unchastity . . . is union
without love," married or not). Attached to a belief in honor and
service, this strict doctrine of male virtue placed tremendous
pressure on men, who represented in a sense the purveyors of
patriarchal respectability. As I have already mentioned, the tenacity of the ideology of Christian manliness is evidenced even
in social sinners like Alec, Troy, Fitzpiers, and Elgar, who feel

genuinely guilty about their moral laxity. Eric Trudgill argues that middle-class men, in fact, involuntarily capitulated to an irrestistible sexual compulsion because of the contradictions at work in patriarchal society. The vice of the middle classes,

> came as a consequence of the constraints of respectability, its repressive indoctrination, its excessively idealized views of marriage and all that that involved: to stigmatize as hypocrites men who were more like casualties of prudery would be to adopt the logic of Butler's *Erewhon*, where illness is a crime. Above all, much Victorian vice exhibited a degree of shame and guilt that would surely abate the censure of all but the most self-righteous of moralists. Considering the easy accessibility of the whore, considering the many rationalizations of misconduct that were available . . . it is remarkable how vigorously many Victorians struggled against indulgence in immorality. (1976, 131)

Shaped by such ideological contradictions of "purity" and "experience," Hardy's upright and prudent heroes are doomed to witness the corruption of an impossible masculine code, in effect, to live out its futility. Again, Angel Clare is a convenient touchstone for the "bad fellow" opposite; he is not effeminate, but strong-willed and physically attractive, a man eager to sacrifice himself (and, unfortunately, others) to support his unreasonable idealizations of what constitutes morality. Above all, he is in his own mind consistent, and to Tess, "His consistency was, indeed, too cruel" (313). This aspect of Angel, his unwavering faithfulness to ideals, is shared by Boldwood, who is steadfastly controlled by a feminine *idée fixe*, and by Giles Winterborne, an inordinantly humble "solid-going fellow" (334). The frustration of masculine love and spiritual generosity—and this is so clear in Angel's case—is caused by just this strict adherence to Christian spiritual ideology that crowds out the possibilities of living a life within the body, or I should say, the reality of the body. In an essay on "manly love and Victorian society," Jeffrey Richards goes so far as to say that it is difficult for twentieth-century readers to fully appreciate "the strength and extent of traditional Christian teaching" on the subject of sex:

> namely that sex interferes with the true vocation of man—the search for spiritual perfection. That is why Christian teaching exalted celibacy and virginity as the highest states of human existence and it is always within that context that we must see the true manly love which passes the love of women. . . . The love of women, with its

inevitable sexual and reproductive element, cannot avoid inferiority within that absolute scale of values. (1987, 93)

Hardy almost certainly understood the limitations within this Christian code of physical purity and spiritual excellence. "Some might risk the odd paradox that with more animalism [Angel] would have been the nobler man," says the narrator of *Tess* (315), for "Clare's love was . . . ethereal to a fault." Nevertheless, he has forcefulness of character, even though his energy is directed oppositely from the sensual conquests of Alec, Troy, or Fitzpiers. Tess "was appalled by the determination revealed in the depths of this gentle being she had married—the will to subdue the grosser to the subtler emotions, the substance to the conception, the flesh to the spirit. Propensities, tendencies, habits . . . were as dead leaves upon the tyrannous winds of his imaginative ascendancy" (316).

"Tyrannous" is a key word, and on one level implies Angel's tyranny over Tess, but the tyranny of men's imaginations over the reality of their lives holds, I think, a more penetrating meaning. Their imaginative renderings of a "well-beloved" and of themselves as romantic rescuers imprison and incapacitate Angel, Boldwood, and Giles. They are, like their less virtuous counterparts, unable to conceive any genuine, broadened vision of the sexual other. Ultimately, they really are unable to act beyond their obsessions. Their idealizations of individual women evolve into a watchful possessiveness, itself an orderly progression of male emotions within patriarchal society, the conventionality of which is apparent in the variety of contemporary responses to Angel's rejection of Tess, though he had been no more chaste than she had. Hardy remarked to Raymond Blathwayt in 1892, that "I have had many letters from men who say they would have done exactly as he did."[3] Apparently there is nothing so abominable about behavior that upholds the double standard in a male-dominated society—indeed, Angel is positively the voice of the masculine public, for despite his professed modernity, he is restricted by old ideas about sexuality. This, says Hardy, "is a deeper shade than the shade which Angel Clare perceived, namely, the shade of his own limitations. With all his attempted independence of judgment, this advanced and well-meaning young man, a sample product of the last five-and-twenty years, was yet a slave to custom and conventionality."[4] Like Reuben Elgar, Angel is "a man of his time," yet he is still oppressed by Victorian sexual orthodoxy.

Angel's spirituality, his consistency and control, and his pretense of moral correctness are counterparts to Alec's sensuality, uncontrolled passions, and moral indifference, and these distinctions largely define the split male psyche in late-century England. What I wish to emphasize is that even Angel and Hardy's other passive heroes are not organically chaste. I do not completely agree with Guerard in respect of the sexlessness of these characters, their "temperamental impotence" (1949, 115), for they do possess a latent virility that ignites their imaginations, if not their deeds. Significantly, the final actions of Boldwood and Winterborne reveal how much they have been harassed by self-enforced sexual repression—they are capable only of perverse chivalry and self-destructive valor.

In *Far from the Madding Crowd* and *The Woodlanders* (1889), Hardy shows the disintegrating male psyche overconditioned by Victorian values of continence and fidelity, and the idealization of women as untouchably pure aesthetic objects. Boldwood and Giles Winterborne are obsessively chaste and passionately devoted lovers whose sexual hesitancy and inexperience typify the contradictions inherent in nineteenth-century masculinity, that is, self-sacrifice and sexual postponement are manly virtues, but when pathologically obeyed create "monsters of affection," gentlemen whose moral rectitude limits their potential for sexual self-knowledge. It must also be remembered that such limitations were built into men's identities. One of the most striking contradictions within late-Victorian culture is that a preoccupation with the ego coexisted with an anxious reluctance to expose one's true self.

In *The Private Papers of Henry Ryecroft*, Gissing's "author at grass" glibly refers to "the natural difficulty of an Englishman in revealing his true self save under the most favorable circumstances," even admitting that he himself is "not quite a representative Englishman; my self-consciousness, my meditative habit of mind, rather dim my national and social characteristics" (114). Yet you have at this time novelists—such as Gissing and Hardy and Meredith—who are centrally occupied with "the liberation of the modern ego" (Stone 1972, 37). For some men, like Boldwood, Angel, and Giles, such liberation involves shaking off tenacious ideological chains that have bound men in a contorted moral posture, that, significantly, patriarchal culture has created and that these men themselves have (with the exception of Clare) unquestioningly adopted. The English Gentleman is an institution with a long history, from the medieval knight errant and the cavalier, to the romantic's nostalgia for aristocratic excellence and the Victorian's emphasis on prudence, fortitude, and character—the composite gentleman who, says Andrew Tolson, remains "morally if not politically, at the summit of civilization. His manners, his sense of 'fairness,' his devotion to 'duty' and 'service' together make up a socially legitimate character type" (1977, 39). But legitimacy has its limitations. Boldwood, for example, is considered a good catch by respectable young ladies partly because he is so legitimate (and apparently harmless), but his particular code of civility has contributed to a repressed and distorted personality. Giles, too, is a taciturn, courteous, and hard-working young man, but these socialized gentlemanly traits (though he is not well-born, he is gentlemanly in the moral sense) correspond with a self-deprecation that is also psychologically crippling.[5] Andrew Tolson aptly describes institutional masculinity as "an internally-woven fabric; inside which a single-minded little man, restlessly struggling, spins his own cocoon" (39).

The shell Hardy's men build around themselves, and the immobility inherent in it, is not induced by a fear of women. Male passivity is not a response to female aggression, to the predatory, self-confident New Woman who makes male heroism problematic at the end of the century.[6] Certainly Grace Melbury is not very intimidating, and however capricious, Bathsheba is hardly a virago. A. O. J. Cockshut, in *Man and Woman: A Study of Love and the Novel, 1740–1940,* correctly states that by the 1880s novelists are dealing with a society "in which sexual roles have been to an astonishing extent reversed" (1978, 132). I think he appropriately applies this reversal to Gissing's characterization:

> Just as we have this female equivalent of the strong, brutal male, so in a different social setting, does Gissing present us with a feminine version of the *ideé reçue* of male superiority in strength, intellect, education, sheer effectiveness in the world. Gone is the old Dickensian and Ruskinian kind of feminine superiority, the moral superiority of the angel in the house. In books like *Born in Exile* (1892) or *The Crown of Life* (1899), it is the woman who is strong, who has an assured position in the world, who can consider the question of marriage coolly on its merits. The men are the fond, weak yearners, who are unspeakably grateful for a smile or a glance. After proposing marriage, Godwin Peak, in *Born in Exile,* is characteristic of a whole group of Gissing's male protagonists when he says: " 'Such a piece of recklessness deserves no answer.' " (1978, 131–32)

There are parallels between this type of male protagonist in Gissing, and Hardy's passive-addictive men, but the female counterpart in Hardy is not really strong and self-assured—only perceived to be that way by men. In fact, Bathsheba and Grace Melbury (and Elfride Swancourt and Sue Bridehead) are impulsive, sexually confused women, not intrepid goddesses. They do not even have the benefit of great wealth or social prestige, like Sidwell Warricombe in *Born in Exile,* for actually it is Godwin Peak's ambition to jump class barriers that makes his proposal so presumptuous. The frantic ardor of Boldwood and Giles is entirely disproportionate to the heroine's merits. In *Far from the Madding Crowd* and *The Woodlanders,* Hardy is not occupied with male victimization, nor, exactly, with sexual pathology. The focus of Ruth Milberg-Kaye's *Thomas Hardy: Myths of Sexuality* (1983) is just this "obsessional pattern" in the novels—she wants to get to the "obsessive Hardy" and learn the "unconscious intention" behind his works, which she finds centered in erotic relationships. Milberg-Kaye is not completely convincing because her argument, heavily Freudian and Jungian, takes no account of the cultural myths surrounding Victorian women and their sexuality—myths Hardy was not sufficiently ahead of his time to completely discredit or ignore. The cultural myths surrounding men also play a predictably essential part in masculine characterization. If there is anything obsessive about Angel, Boldwood, and Winterborne (and I do not deny that there is), it is acceptably reinforced by social and moral conventions. Their continence is a reflex, and their blind devotion is a casualty of the ethos of Christian manliness.

According to Michael Millgate's biography, Hardy was "obsessed throughout his life by the struggle between body and soul." In a comment on W. E. Henley's poem "Invictus," Hardy once declared, "No man is master of his soul; the flesh is master of it!" (1982, 295). In their various studies, Steven Marcus, Ronald Pearsall, Trudgill, and Peter Gay review the pervasiveness of Hardy's particular "obsession" throughout Victorian society as a whole. Their discussions of Victorian sexual repression and the pressures both men and women were under to "subdue the flesh" encompass more detail than I need to go into here. Still, Boldwood and Winterborne are examples of men who direct their energies inward, and, ironically, so are Hardy's seducers, who (for the most part) exert their wills by acting on, not by analyzing, their motives. Thus the masculine will is anti-introspective;

it contributes to male sexual suppression even while indulging sexual desires. Marcus's explanation of the essential inversion of male self-awareness supports my impression of the alienation of Hardy's men from their own sexuality. "For although the will is a form of consciousness and is consciously employed," says Marcus,

> its energies have historically been directed against consciousness itself—against intellect, self-examination, curiosity. Will is, in other words, a controlled consciousness which often contains within itself a fear of consciousness. (1964, 24)

In *Madding Crowd* and *The Woodlanders*, Hardy taps into this essential paradox: Boldwood and Giles are not sexless or functionally sterile, but sexual and willful men whose consciousness is conditioned by an impulse toward anticonsciousness, which is further exploited and regulated by institutionalized masculinity. In other words, their lack of self-understanding is intrinsically linked to their assumptions about gender roles in their society. "In the masculine world there is no room for introspection," claims Andrew Tolson (1977, 86), and the American writer Rafford Pyke wrote in 1902 that the average male was curiously deficient in self-analysis. That a man can even make such a statement indicates that by the 1880s and 1890s male self-knowledge had become a critical issue, especially where sexual matters were concerned. Fraser Harrison points out that men who had "previously been accustomed to treating their sexual instincts as an aspect of themselves that was best suppressed and forgotten" are now being compelled by the feminist debate to "expose and explore that part of their being which they had learnt to hide and shackle," and that "men who sought the fulfillment of their sexuality set themselves a painful and demanding task, so demanding indeed that many abandoned the attempt in despair" (1978, 133). Boldwood and Giles seem initially to have surrendered up their troublesome sexuality, sublimating those energies into other activities, but falling in love lifts the veil from their sexual selves and introduces a new element of psychological tension into their characters. Their struggle to adapt their sexual desires to a much obeyed doctrine of continence and suppression adds an almost adolescent *bildung* to the pastoral love story.

Boldwood is not the hero of *Far from the Madding Crowd*. His character defies compartmentalization in the customary classification of Hardy's "types," for he is neither a seducer (Alec, Troy, Fitzpiers, Wildeve) nor a saint (Oak, Venn, Giles, Yeobright). His tragedy is close to Michael Henchard's, and both men are volcanoes beneath the surface, but there is more pathos than tragedy in Boldwood's downfall. he is as psychologically complex as Jocelyn Pierston in *The Well-Beloved*, but not as sophisticated and self-aware. He is, to me, the most intimidating man in any of Hardy's novels because he is so determined, yet at the same time so reckless—indeed, his self-subdual is more threatening than Alec d'Urberville's self-indulgence. In Boldwood, Hardy exposes the vice and destructiveness in masculine restraint and the potential power of subdued sexual consciousness when it is disturbed into awareness.

Ian Ousby sees Boldwood (and Troy, for that matter) as the victim of his own complexities. The character's apparent self-discipline conceals turbulent passions so that Boldwood really does seem to represent a merging of the Alec/Angel duality. "With the receipt of Bathsheba's provocative valentine," explains Ousby, "he moves from one polar opposite to the other; the stoic misogynist becomes a passionate lover, the ascetic a sensualist" (1981, 35). His love for Bathsheba is entirely manufactured from an imagined ideal that is quite detached from reality: "His downfall . . . demonstrates not women's maliciously exercised power over men but rather the power of the mere idea of women over men. It shows men's capacity for destroying themselves by their own volatile and irreconcilable impulses" (Ousby 1981, 36). This reading comes closest to my own impressions about the character and about the personal tensions Hardy seems to have located there.

What Ousby does not address, however, and what I find most interesting, is that the male possessive "instinct" and the propensity for sexual fixations is, in Boldwood, the emotional crisis of his life—a sexual awakening in middle age. Hardy repeatedly emphasizes the desperation of male desire when past the flirtations of youth, a subject he will treat more fully almost twenty years later in *The Well-Beloved*, and which Gissing analyzes in *Sleeping Fires* as a kind of successful case study in how not to do it. Even Bathsheba is stunned by Boldwood's mature seriousness: "How was I to know that what is a pastime to all other men was death to you?" she says (158). And she has a point, especially in that physically and socially Boldwood does not appear very vulnerable. He is "the nearest approach to aristocracy in the parish" (94). Physically, he is described as tall, dark, Roman-esque, square-framed, a man "in the climax of life, with his bronzed Roman face and fine frame" (159). It is characteristic of Hardy to impressionistically describe figures, forms, and shapes perceived from a distance, but the frequency in which he uses this technique in describing Boldwood suggests an intentional evocation of a dim but powerful presence.[7] At the sheep-shear-ing, for example, "Nobody seemed to have perceived his entry, but there he certainly was. Boldwood always carried with him a social atmosphere of his own, which everybody felt who came near him" (116); at the malthouse "a shade darkened the door" (88), he had mysteriously "withdrawn into the encircling dust" (123), he is like "an unhappy Shade" (182), "a figure" against "the blazing sky . . . like the black snuff in the midst of a candle-flame" (82). The imagery surrounding him is dark, powerful, Byronic, and essentially masculine. And yet, ironically, the re-ceipt of a frivolous valentine disturbs "the symmetry of his exis-tence" and puts him in a state of "nervous excitability" (80, 81). The gentle yeoman, whose stable is "his almonry and cloister," "the celibate" who walks and meditates in solitude, is jolted into confrontation with sensuous existence—with his *own* sexuality, not Bathsheba's for he is sexually aroused before he even notices her. Like a sort of agricultural Kurtz, Boldwood looks into his suppressed soul and finds that the virility and aggressiveness of institutionalized masculine "nature" has infiltrated the placid, self-denying gentleman.

And it is like an awakening, a coming into consciousness; the whole process requires a boldness in which the brooding farmer is quite unpracticed. Hardy compares Boldwood to Adam waking from a deep sleep, "and behold! there was Eve" (93). Hardy's "Adam," though, doesn't know quite what to do with his compli-cated helpmate. Unlike experienced men, Boldwood has never contemplated Woman. He does not even know if Bathsheba is considered handsome, and has to ask a neighbor at the mar-ketplace if she is very much noticed. Compared to Troy, whose almost first words to Bathsheba are about her face, Boldwood is singularly naive. The narrator skillfully moves in and out of Boldwood's consciousness, effectively illuminating the move-ment of his mind in participation with objective reality. He watches Bathsheba, like so many men watch women in Hardy, but humanly, wonderingly—he is not Fitzpiers peering over a hedge at Grace Melbury, or Gabriel Oak spying on Bathsheba's creative horsemanship in the woods. The scene is one of the most sympathetic pictures of Boldwood's essential innocence and vulnerability:

> Boldwood looked at her—not slily, critically, or understandingly, but blankly at gaze, in the way a reaper looks up at a passing train—as something foreign to his element, and but dimly understood. To Boldwood women had been remote phenomena rather than necessary complements. . . .
>
> He saw her black hair, her correct facial curves and profile, and the roundness of her chin and throat. He saw then the side of her eyelids, eyes, and lashes, and the shape of her ear. Next he noticed her figure, her skirt, and the very soles of her shoes.
>
> . . . His heart began to move within him. Boldwood, it must be remembered, though forty years of age, had never before inspected a woman with the very center and force of his glance; they had struck upon all his senses at wide angles. (93)

The impression here is that Boldwood is awakened to female beauty and sexuality, but subsequent episodes reveal that he is struck less by Bathsheba than by what the idea of Bathsheba has stirred in himself. In fact, he reevaluates his entire life and finds he has lived wrongly, if not unnaturally—"I am now forty-one years old. . . . I may have been called a confirmed bachelor, and I was a confirmed bachelor. . . . But we all change, and my change, in this matter, came with seeing you. I have felt lately, more and more, that my present way of living is bad in every respect" (100). Restraint and celibacy have become "bad" to him, an interesting moral reversal in mid-life. Still, Boldwood is not on the road toward profligacy. He is confirmed in the gentlemanly arts of winning a woman properly, and his clumsy if passionate courtesy is diametrically opposed to Troy's unscrupulous strategies. Boldwood's techniques are inept but sincere: "I wish I could say courteous flatteries to you . . . and put my rugged feeling into a graceful shape: but I have neither power nor patience to learn such things," he says. "Ah! I wish I knew how to win you!" (100–1).

He does not know how to make love, so he blunders the same way Oak does in the beginning of the novel, and the way Giles does in wooing Grace with an excess of gentlemanliness that is a handicap placed against the win-her-at-any-cost mentality of the less patient seducer. Although Oak, for example, passionately tells Bathsheba he will keep wanting her until he dies, he also admits that it is too bad she has no dowry—thus, "Farmer Oak had one-and-a-half Christian characteristics too many to succeed with Bathsheba: his humility, and a superfluous moiety of honesty" (29). He is also too self-respecting and fair-minded to press her; like Giles Winterborne, he surrenders to a more genteel rival instead of obeying the "brute instinct." Because Oak is "thoroughly convinced of the impossibility of his own suit, a high resolve constrained him not to injure that of another. This is a lover's most stoical virtue, as the lack of it is a lover's most venial sin" (105). Boldwood is incapable of the characteristic Oak stoicism. Bathsheba begs him to "be neutral," and he tells her himself, "I am no stoic" (102, 157). His gentlemanly lovemaking has an urgency to it that more than once frightens Bathsheba. Susan Beegel, in an excellent essay about male sexual symbolism and sexual morbidity in *Far from the Madding Crowd*, correctly points out that the marriage Boldwood offers Bathsheba is one of entombment and suffocation ("I will protect and cherish you with all my strength," he says. "You shall never have so much as to look out of doors.") She finally accepts his last proposal partly because she is hounded. Boldwood's persistency brings him closer to success than his basic merits as a devoted husband and provider. Certainly he is, as I have suggested, an incompetent lover. Indeed, his "fatal omission" is that he had never once told Bathsheba she was beautiful, a stock line for Sergeant Troy, and a fundamental in most masculine marriage maneuvers, especially since female vanity is held to be an undisputed truth in patriarchal society (which, incidentally, encourages it). Hardy says quite openly: "The wondrous power of flattery in *passados* at women is a perception so universal as to be remarked upon by many people almost as automatically as they repeat a proverb" (132). Yet Boldwood seems insensible to the strength of the compliment—which is at least less cynical than Troy's observation that in dealing with womankind, the only alternative to flattering is cursing and swearing. But Boldwood no longer really sees Bathsheba at all, and the focus of his obsession is not so much getting her sexually as it is finding some legitimate outlet for a volcanic passion he is, quite literally, afraid and ashamed of. "I am beyond myself about this, and am mad," he tells her (157), yet he cannot bear to think of going back to how he was before the fatal valentine, living in "cold darkness." The loss of Bathsheba (though he admits, ironically, "I never had you") is the tragedy of Boldwood's life.

Hardy does not create a romantic picture of cruel heartbreak and disappointed young love, nor of dignified, if hopeful, resolution, such as Langley exhibits in *Sleeping Fires*, a novel I will look more closely at later. Boldwood is simply an exposed and humiliated middle-aged man. "As for me, I had better go somewhere alone, and hide—and pray. I loved a woman once. I am now ashamed. When I am dead they'll say, Miserable love-sick man that he was. . . . . Shame upon him—shame!" (160) His impulsive urge to "hide—and pray" suggests Boldwood's guilt at his own desires and fantasies. He is both ashamed and outraged because Bathsheba has disappointed his vision of feminine modesty and prudence. "Whilst I would have given worlds to touch your hand, you have let a rake come in without right or ceremony and—kiss you! Heaven's mercy—kiss you!" (160). Very quickly, the humiliated man is transformed unconsciously into the threatening villain, the opponent of the chivalric defender of feminine virtue. Hardy's rhetoric here is certainly evocative of the knightly code—Bathsheba calls Boldwood "unmanly" and says, "I have nobody in the world to fight my battles for me; but no mercy is shown" (160). Because Boldwood jealously sees Troy as the enemy, he furiously vows to "horsewhip the untimely stripling for this reckless theft of my one delight" (161), but at this point it is difficult to feel convinced that Boldwood has found anything delightful about Bathsheba, love, or sexual excitement. If his masculine experience has been enlarged or enhanced at all by this passion, it is in the direction of his capacity to persevere; Boldwood is, like Clare, cruel in his consistency. "Where there is much bias there must be some narrowness," the narrator says. "We discern a grand force in the lover which he lacks whilst a free man; but there is a breadth of vision in the free man which in the lover we vainly seek" (177).

Certainly Angel Clare lacks breadth of vision. He and Boldwood are like the ironically named Henry Knight in *A Pair of Blue Eyes* (1873), "who had missed his mark by excessive aiming" (392).[8] Boldwood's single-mindedness—like Angel's and Winterborne's—is the root of his tragedy. His "immobility" and "steadiness" (185) are worse than a collapse, and betray "an expression deeper than a cry," comparable to Angel, "calm and cold, his small compressed mouth indexing his powers of self-control, his face wearing still that terrible sterile expression" (*Tess*, 305). Both men are resisting and suppressing their inability to accept the accidents and frustrations of sexual reality, explaining their defeat as, on the one hand, dishonesty and betrayal, and on the other, irrepressible ardor. Boldwood's inexperience with the complexities and vagaries of sexual love leave him foundering in the realm of imagination only; he cannot see beyond his

ideal, beyond his great hope. He cannot even see Bathsheba as a
particular woman in a particular predicament—like Tess, who
turns out to be "another woman in your shape" (*Tess*, 255).
Boldwood wonders about an abstraction: "Does a woman keep
her promise?" (276). He, in effect, creates a fiction: "In a locked
closet was now discovered an extraordinary collection of arti-
cles. . . . They were all carefully packed in paper, and each pack-
age was labelled 'Bathsheba Boldwood,' a date being subjoined
six years in advance in every instance" (294). Of course the
fiction is not just about Bathsheba for Boldwood has cast himself
in the role of Bathsheba's husband, protector, provider, and the
proprietor of her sexuality perfectly symbolized by the silks,
satins, and velvets he has so tenderly packed away.

In the creation of Boldwood, Hardy exposes the perversity and
danger in masculine fidelity to a sexual ideal—for Angel, the
victim is Tess; for Boldwood, it is his rival and himself. Men's
incapacity to distance themselves from their own moral dogmas
reflects a latent uneasiness with their own sexuality. It is a fear of
powerlessness over their own mysterious sexual nature, as well
as over the uncategorizable Other. George Meredith sees such
men as callous, tyrannical, and blind, because like Percy Dacier,
the finely bred Englishman in *Diana of the Crossways* (1889),
they prefer the "right worshipful heroine of Romance" to the
"flecked heroine of reality" (294–95). Hardy himself confessed to
having "no great liking for the perfect woman of fiction," adding,
"but this may be for purely artistic reasons" (Millgate 1982, 168).
The man who takes his Christian gentlemanliness to an abnormal extreme is a self-constructed paragon of masculinity, the
right worshipful hero of his own life. He fails to see the fic-
tionality of his fiction, not understanding that there is a degree of
madness in chaste consistency as well as in moral deviance.

Gissing also deals with masculine honor, sexual experience,
and maturity in a thirty-thousand-word novella that manages to
come across as both sensible and sympathetic despite occasional
lapses in the plot. Written between January and March 1895,
Sleeping Fires seems imbedded with a pointed lesson about
sexual self-respect, the hazards of moral pedantry, and the trap of
romantic love. Forty-two-year-old Edmund Langley is a case
study in masculine assertiveness, but more important, he is a
man who actually learns from his mistakes. After his "perverse
heroism" (19) causes the loss of the woman he loves at the age of
twenty-six, Langley undergoes a sexual awakening similar to
Boldwood's, when he again meets Agnes Forrest (now Lady Re-

vill) sixteen years later under stirring and extraordinary circumstances. Langley regrets the "imbecile hesitation" and moral conscientiousness that compelled him to confess his youthful sins to Agnes's father (who responds understandingly enough—"well, a young man is a young man"), thereby risking rejection of his suit. "I was absurd, when I thought myself nobly honest," he reflects, and he eventually tells Agnes, "If I had been bolder, then, how different our lives! I ought not to have accepted your refusal" (85, 89). Not taking no for an answer is certainly Boldwood's method. Both middle-aged men feel a sexual potency that is "yet another step in that reasonable unrest of manhood which had come upon him like an awakening after sluggish sleep" (*Sleeping Fires*, 32). Amazed at himself, Langley feels as desperate as a twenty-year-old, with "so much more of resolute manhood than in the prime of youth" (76). Like Boldwood, he is almost violent in his persistence, but finally, Gissing's more sanguine hero escapes the danger of creating a "Bathsheba Boldwood," offering Agnes only "a mere unheraldic mortal," an exchange of "the style of chivalry for a bourgeois prefix" (97). Indeed, his thirty-seven-year-old "goddess" is prosaically described as being like most wealthy women her age, well-preserved, even discomposing to men, but with a certain "loss of sweetness." Male passion in middle age, Gissing suggests, can and should be tempered with reasonable objectivity (a lesson, by the way, Hardy's Jocelyn Pierston does not learn until he is past sixty); love should take place "in the world of realities" that need not necessarily be either "a life of sluggish respectability" or "castles in the air" (100, 87, 95). As Hardy puts it at the end of *Far from the Madding Crowd*, "the romance growing up in the interstices of a mass of hard prosaic reality" (303) is firmer and more fulfilling than a beautiful obsession. Hardy and Gissing (at least in this novella) resemble Meredith in their common-sense approach to uncommon passions.

Meredith, however, is certainly more sage. Though not quite as blunt as *The Egoist, Diana of the Crossways* is an interesting study of socialized masculinity. Almost all the male characters are outwardly impeccable English gentlemen who each have their faults, including the faithful and heroic Thomas Redworth, a character Meredith approves of, but who nevertheless has his critics in the novel. "Mr. Redworth," according to Emma Dunstan, "was manly and trustworthy: of the finest Saxon type in build and in character. He had great qualities, and his excess of scrupulousness was most pitiable" (49). He is pitiable to women, even strong and feminist-leaning women like Diana, who have a desire to depend on a man of character—a wish, whether innate or superficial, to relinquish themselves to masculine strength. In *Love and the Woman Question in Victorian Literature*, Kathleen Blake discusses "male dominance as a fact and as a wish" in Gissing's novels, particularly *The Odd Women*. "There is a difference between the theory of the prevailing will in men and the actuality," she explains, citing the delusiveness of the idea of male strength and authority as having a "ruinous impact on the relations between the sexes" (1983, 82–86). *The Odd Women* gives particular insight into masculine diffidence for the men in the novel, with the exception of Everard Barfoot, are essentially like Boldwood—a combination of timidity and rashness. They also bear a marked resemblance to the "hero" of *The Woodlanders*.

A comparison of *The Woodlanders*, published in 1887, and *Far from the Madding Crowd*, serialized some fourteen years earlier, may at first seem incongruous, especially considering how much more complex are the issues treated in the later novels such as *Tess* and *Jude*. In fact, *The Woodlanders* and *Madding Crowd* are closely linked. Michael Millgate explains how contemporary reviewers of *The Woodlanders* suggested that the new novel was a reworking of the earlier story, which has some bearing upon Hardy's statement (in *Early Life*) that when he began writing in November 1885 he went back to his "original plot". "If," says Millgate,

> that plot dated from as far back as 1875 when . . . he put aside "a woodland story he had thought of" in order to write *The Hand of Ethelberta*, then it would not only account for features otherwise surprising in a novel published between *The Mayor of Casterbridge* and *Tess of the d'Urbervilles* but allow the story to be thought of as combining the pastoral material and the intricate plotting characteristic of the early novels with the greater maturity of technique and tone which marks the later works. (1971, 249–50)

Analogies between the characters in both novels, though, are not clear-cut. Giles Winterborne, for example, seems at first to have less in common with the impetuosity of Boldwood than with Oak's steadfastness. But Giles's masculine valor is of a different nature than Oak's, whose common sense would hardly condone a slavish adherence to notions of propriety that, under the circumstances, are dangerous nonsense.

Oak is one of Hardy's rare survivors; his sterling character and self-respect absolutely forbid him to idolize any woman or jeopardize his dignity for the sake of an infatuation. More important is Oak's sexual equilibrium: he is Hardy's version of the male ideal, perfectly balanced between the flesh and the spirit—his features "adhered throughout to their form so exactly to the middle line of the beauty of St. John and the ugliness of Judas Iscariot" (10). Even his "toilet" is "of a nicely-adjusted kind . . . of a degree between fine-market-day and wet-Sunday selection" (24). Unlike Boldwood, Oak's erotic adventures begin at the perfect time of life:

> He was at the brightest period of masculine growth, for his intellect and his emotions were clearly separated: he had passed the time during which the influences of youth indiscriminately mingles them in the character of impulse, and he had not yet arrived at the stage wherein they become united again, in the character of prejudice, by the influence of a wife and a family. (3)

He has had, probably, no sexual experience—indeed, Oak has "a quiet modesty that would have become a vestal" (8), but he is by no means effeminate: "His height and breadth would have been sufficient to make his presence imposing, had they been exhibited with due consideration" (8). Though his "special power . . . was static," he "could do a thing with as mercurial a dash as can the men of towns" when he wants to (13). In effect, Hardy is describing a rustic Lancelot: pure, dutiful, strong, modest.[9] Not only does he rescue the damsel in distress when her ricks are on fire, her sheep are dying, and her corn is threatened by the storm, but he maintains a flame of passion for Bathsheba that is neither as combustible nor as extinguishable as the sexual desires of Hardy's rakes and gallants. Oak is masculine symmetry, not masculine extremity, and so, unlike Angel or Boldwood, represents the genuine hero, or man of character.[10]

Giles Winterborne is a sort of spurious version of Oakian manliness, inauthentic because his masculinity is imbalanced and extreme. In many ways he is an attractive character, "Autumn's very brother," so close to the pulse of the woodlands that his planting ensures straight, healthy growth. Like Oak, Winterborne bears up bravely under adversity; indeed, he probably would have survived a great deal of bad luck if he were not so pitifully scrupulous and simple. The tragedy is that Giles errs in the opposite way from Boldwood—he is too quick to give up, rather

than too determined to persevere—without seeing that Grace is
by no means immovable or indifferent. "Giles, if you had only
shown half the boldness before I married that you show now, you
would have carried me off for your own, first instead of second,"
she tells him (356). Grace, in fact, admits to herself that Giles's
diffidence is the only flaw in an otherwise noble character. When
Fitzpiers teases her about "an admirer," she says he perhaps has
all the cardinal virtues, though she does not know them precisely:

> "You unconsciously practice them, Miss Melbury, which is better.
> According to Schleiermacher they are Self-Control, Perseverance,
> Wisdom, and Love; and his is the best list I know."
> "I am afraid poor—" She was going to say that she feared Winter-
> borne . . . had not much perseverance, though he had all the other
> three; but she determined to go no further in this direction and was
> silent. (191)

Giles's habit of "reserve and restraint" and his tendency to
"keep emotion suspended" cannot compete with "the handsome,
coercive, irresistible Fitzpiers" (59, 74, 216). Giles is not only a
hesitant lover, but an awkward one, who says the wrong things at
the wrong time, and whose "self-deprecatory sense of living on a
much smaller scale" than Grace causes painful misunderstand-
ings. His Christmas party is a fiasco, he unwittingly bids against
Melbury at the timber sale, and he stupidly overstays his wel-
come at Melbury's home after the purchase of the mare for Grace.
His self-forgetfulness is the reverse of male self-centeredness. As
Guerard puts it, "generous self-denial can cause as much mischief as egoism" (117). Although he nobly retires into the background after Grace marries Fitzpiers, Winterborne is not above
subtle remarks about the past or mischievous hints about the
present. He is not jealous or malicious, merely honest (if not
tactful). It is this ingenuousness that Grace finds a refreshing
contrast to her husband. Giles's closeness to nature, his innocence, make him appear in her imagination as a pastoral hero:
"another being, impersonating chivalrous and undiluted manliness, had arisen out of the earth ready to her hand" (261). But
he is, significantly, only an impersonator; Giles is rough-hewn
manliness, and when he unpremeditatedly caresses a flower
Grace wears in her bosom, she must reproach him for taking a
liberty. "I don't know what I am coming to!" he exclaims sav-
agely. "Ah—I was not once like this!" His vexation is similar to

Boldwood's sense of being unnerved by a sexual desire that he must suppress, and is a clue to how shocked these men are at their own impulses. They do feel as though they are not themselves. Giles is also like Angel Clare, "a man with a conscience," whose spirituality strives to resist "grosser nature." When Grace permits him to kiss her, Winterborne's struggle with himself is almost promethean:

> "O Heaven!" groaned Winterborne to himself. His head was turned askance as he still resolutely regarded the ground. For the last several minutes he had seen this *great temptation* approaching him in *regular siege*: and now it had come. The *wrong, the social sin,* of now taking advantage of the offer of her lips, had a magnitude in the eyes of one whose life had been so primitive, so ruled by household laws as Giles's, which can hardly be explained. . . .
>
> Winterborne, though *fighting valiantly* against himself all the while—though he would have protected Grace's good repute as the apple of his eye, was a man; and as Desdemona said, men are not gods. In face of the *agonizing seductiveness* shown by her, in her unenlightened school-girl simplicity about the laws and ordinances, he betrayed *a man's weakness*. . . . [He] gave way to *the temptation*, not withstanding that he perfectly well knew her to be wedded irrevocably to Fitzpiers. (355; my emphasis)

Such melodramatic scrupulousness may seem to us an almost comical description of Victorian prudery, but Hardy is not exaggerating the typical Victorian guilt a man like Winterborne could have felt in such a situation. Giles's "primitive" beliefs in the susceptibility of a woman's reputation and his own struggle to "reduce his former passion to a docile friendship" (340) are taken to the worst extreme when he sacrifices his life for Grace in a series of scenes that brings to mind the story of Beauty and the Beast. Grace begins to imagine Giles as an erotic diety even before she seeks his protection, when he is still "invisible" to her:

> She saw nothing of Winterborne during the days of her recovery; and perhaps on that account her fancy wove about him a more romantic tissue than it could have done if he had stood before her with all the specks and flaws inseparable from concrete humanity. He rose upon her memory as the fruit-god and the wood-god in alteration: sometimes leafy and smeared with green lichen . . . sometimes cider-stained and starred with apple-pips. (341)

When Grace begins to view Giles as "a man whom she had wronged," he is invested in her imagination with "a real touch of sublimity" (277). Hardy's list of masculine virtues seems purposeful, even when interpreted as the sentimental awakening of a young woman who realizes she has married the wrong person: "Honesty, goodness, manliness, tenderness, devotion, for her only existed in their purity now in the breast of unvarnished men; and here was one who had manifested such towards her from his youth up" (276). Even Gabriel Oak does not receive such a romanticized catalog of homage. But despite Grace's tender feelings of love and remorse, Winterborne is not a picture of equipoised male sexuality, perfectly neutralized or undiluted. After Giles's pathetically valorous death, the narrator comments upon more than Grace's narrow orthodoxy by saying, "Her timid morality had, indeed, underrated his chivalry till now" (381). There is an implicit sense that Grace should be forgiven for not seeing the pathology of Giles's "heroism" that Hardy treats with both sympathy and aversion. Giles's "scrupulous delicacy" ends in a self-sacrifice that is sadder because it is wasted—the great irony being that Grace ends up at the Earl of Wessex with Fitzpiers anyway, and so misses a final rendezvous with Marty South at Giles's grave.

The extremity of male continence and consistency in both Boldwood and Winterborne is as destructive as the sexual indulgence of their aggressive male counterparts. Unless a man has the advantage of hindsight combined with the courage of his convictions—a man such as Gissing's Langley—there is less danger in the sexual fall itself than there is in the fear of falling. There is always time for remorse later if a man is driven to do things "when his blood is hot" (Sleeping Fires, 95), and even Langley, it must be pointed out, is no babe in the woods. He regards his desertion of the mother of his son as blameless—"He was not responsible for the girl's lapse of virtue," thinks the young man, and even in his forties he pleads "my youth and manhood—a far more valid excuse" (17, 85).

Boldwood and Giles, sexually inexperienced, their passions repressed, expose their fear of sex with a different kind of self-defending rationality that is not less destructive, in their illusion of control: Giles is "a solid-going fellow," and Boldwood says huskily, "Nothing hurts me. My constitution is an iron one" (198). Their manliness and taciturnity, however, barely conceal their sense of panic when their sexual nature is stimulated by an imaginatively charged conception of a woman. They are further alienated from their own sexuality by a strict adherence to moral conventions, which each man, in his own way, manages to pervert. Each are sad, self-deceiving martyrs who share with Angel Clare the false notion that because he is "singularly free from grossness," he has himself "well in hand" (*Tess*, 257).

Both Gissing and Hardy, then, describe male characters who choose ideologically viable sexual roles—the seducer and the gentleman are both culturally legitimate models—that eventually prove self-destructive, or at the least (in Tarrant's case) self-deceptive. I see the deterioration of the reliable, familiar masculine role as stimulating men's interest in revising the feminine ideal. The subject of chapter 4 is how the male character's fantasy of female perfection exposes a desire to simplify sexual roles by romanticizing them. But men's effort to play the ideal lover to the ideal woman also breaks down, as the protagonists of *The Odd Women* and *The Well-Beloved* come to realize the falsification inherent in the fantasy, and their own inability to live out the romantic role in which they have cast themselves.

4

Modern Romantics: *The Well-Beloved* and *The Odd Women*

It would be hard to name two novels written within one year of each other, by writers whose works are in many ways thematically linked, which are more dissimilar than *The Odd Women* (1893) and *The Well-Beloved* (1892). The titles of both books suggest feminine subject matter, though the novels are as much about men as about women, the male protagonists being mostly occupied with finding their private sexual ideal and living with her happily ever after. Both Jocelyn Pierston and Everard Barfoot end up settling for less, but at least their homely needs are taken care of and they can rest from travel—whether in the world of realities or of romance. The most obvious difference between the novels is that *The Well-Beloved* in Hardy's words, is "a wildly romantic fancy," whereas in *The Odd Women* Gissing declared his focus to be "a study of vulgarism."[1] Yet both novels exemplify the literary dialectic that existed in the last two decades of the century. They are concerned with the role imagination and idealism play in erotic relationships, and with the possibility of preserving a moment of make-believe under the crush of mundane facts.

Hardy and Gissing have different approaches to this theme, and their particular treatment of the romance of reality, and vice versa, proves their originality in addressing one of the central literary debates of the age. As Donald David Stone explains, the split between realism and romance in politics was reflected in a split between realism and romance in the novel:

The mood of the 1880's, John Gross has recently said . . . was marked by "a widespread faltering of Victorian self-confidence, a new edginess and uncertainty about the future." And while many literary critics addressed themselves to the problems of the age in a "mood of determined realism," the more common reaction, exemplified by

Henley and Lang, "was withdrawal, a retreat into nostalgia, exoticism, fine writing, *belles-lettres*." The gap between social and literary criticism, which Arnold had tried to bridge, widened, and the distinction between fiction as a mirror of life and as a distraction from life became more pronounced.[2]

Gissing is clearly on the side of social realism, at least in *The Odd Women*, and Hardy is concerned with a man's retreat into aestheticism. Still, the male protagonists in *The Odd Women* and *The Well-Beloved* are both restlessly in need of "a distraction from life," and each is in pursuit of an erotic relationship that meets his personal standards—one of "reality" and one of "romance". In both novels, the hero's story essentially revolves around the possibility of his discovering the woman who will embody his private fantasy.

The Well-Beloved is about a sculptor who, as a young man, falls in love with one woman (Avice I), and then develops an obsessive pattern of infatuation with her daughter (Avice II) in middle age, and her granddaughter (Avice III) as an old man. Jocelyn Pierston eventually ends up alone and cynical, until a pragmatic marriage in his sixties with the woman who first distracted him from the original Avice. Gissing's novel—which is more densely plotted and problem-oriented than Hardy's—concerns the struggles of "odd" or surplus women in London who must support themselves, and especially the decision for or against marriage that confronts the feminist heroine, Rhoda Nunn. The hero of *The Odd Women* is a misogynist in feminist clothing who loves Rhoda—or, more accurately, loves the rebellious Rhoda he dreams of subduing.

Artistic intention and authorial perspective are translated variously into the attitudes of Jocelyn Pierston and Everard Barfoot toward the opposite sex: Hardy's sculptor is fascinated by the girl/goddess, whereas Gissing's modern gentleman is inclined towards the woman/worker. Yet both men are aware of the complex intersection in feminine nature of innocence and experience, sex and necessity. For example, though he respects her independence and commitment, Barfoot is certainly attentive to Rhoda's sexuality; and Pierston understands that all three Avices, however beautiful, are poor islanders who have to work for a living. The desire for a malleable young thing ("the sultan syndrome," John Fowles calls it)[3] is ultimately stronger than the wish for an intelligent and independent-minded companion, as I will show, and this is not surprising considering the volatile state of sexual relations at the end of the century. Christopher Lasch correctly points out that "as male supremacy becomes ideologically untenable, incapable of justifying itself as protection, men assert their domination more directly, in fantasies and occasionally in acts of raw violence."[4] For Victorian men, the fantasy is split between two types of women, the nymphet and the suffragette, and initially both men in *The Well-Beloved* and *The Odd Women* want some kind of combination—even Pierston, who is disappointed to discover that the second Avice lacks the intellectual spirit of the original.

Hardy pinpoints the masculine desire for female sweetness combined with strength in Edward Springrove's description of the ideal wife, as related to Owen Graye, in *Desperate Remedies*, written some twenty years before *The Well-Beloved*:

> "she must be girlish and artless: yet he would be loth to do without a dash of womanly subtlety, 'tis so piquant. Yes, he said, that must be in her; she must have womanly cleverness. 'And yet I should like her to blush if only a cock-sparrow were to look at her hard,' he said, 'which brings me back to the girl again: and so I flit backwards and forwards. I must have what comes, I suppose,' he said, 'and whatever she may be, thank God she's no worse. However, if he might give a final hint to Providence,' he said, 'a child among pleasures and a woman among pains was the rough outline of his requirement.' " (22)

Something between a flighty Dora Spenlow and a long-suffering Agnes Wickfield, David Copperfield's two wives, seems to have been the fictional ideal here. Gissing and Hardy were preoccupied with the unavailability or lack of such well-balanced girl-women in their personal lives. Gissing, certainly, felt keenly the impossibility of associating with intellectual women of the upper classes. "I am too poor to marry an equal and cannot live alone," he wrote in 1890. "[t]here is no real hope of my ever marrying anyone of the better kind, no *real* hope whatever!" Thus for deeply personal reasons he deplored the socialized insipidity of uneducated women. In the same letter in which Gissing said that, "There will be no social peace until women are intellectually trained very much as men are" (quoted in Chapter 1), he went on to say,

> Among our English emancipated women there is a majority of admirable persons; they have lost no single good quality of their sex, and they have gained enormously on the intellectual (and even on the moral) side by the process of enlightenment, that is to say, brain-

development. I am driven frantic by the crass imbecility of the typical woman. (Young 1961, 110–12, 171)

Along with such professed liberalism, though, Gissing expressed definite fears about the limits of female emancipation. The Gissing character in *Born in Exile*, Godwin Peak, exclaims typically, "I hate emancipated women. Women ought neither to be enlightened nor dogmatic. They ought to be sexual" (119). The novel shows, interestingly, that male ambivalence about feminism is often rooted in men's self-interest and in their anxiety, but the male novelist frequently gives it a loftier name, like Love or Art, that women cannot appreciate. "Woman, *qua* woman, hates abstract thought—hates it. Moreover (and of consequence) she despises every ambition that has not a material end," declares Earwaker in *Born in Exile* (138). A certain type of "materialist" woman—the brave, impoverished feminist who seeks opportunities—is treated with more sympathy (and sanity) in *The Odd Women*, but the male hero of that novel is unable to fuse an old sexual fantasy, the woman beautiful, sexual, and submissive, with a modern one, the woman beautiful, educated, and independent. Barfoot himself becomes a "materialist" by the end of the novel. Incompatible ideals drive even the most imaginative and passionate men back into conventionality, or into reassuring roles that keep the private ideal intact.

Throughout his career Hardy was attracted to accomplished and intellectually sophisticated women. Millgate even claims that Florence Henniker was "the emancipated woman for whom Hardy had long been seeking, an ideal resting place for the well-beloved" (1982, 336). But in *The Well-Beloved*, the artist-lover finds less allure in female intelligence than in beauty and girlish innocence, even though before and during the composition of the serial, Hardy was in the company of mature and accomplished London hostesses, not Wessex maidens (Millgate 1982, 296–98, 328–33). The fantasy of Hardy's life was, significantly, based partly on graceful intellectual companionship as well as sexual fulfillment. By 1889, Hardy

was looking quite deliberately outside his marriage for emotional satisfaction, and potentially for sexual satisfaction. Like many men, Hardy enjoyed the public appearance of sexual privilege almost as much as its actual exercise, and although there is no evidence, and little likelihood, that his adventures went to the point, or even within the range, of adultery, he kept only the slackest reins on his fantasy life at this time—as *The Well-Beloved* was to indicate—and made the most of his many opportunities to be in the company of handsome women and receive their attention and admiration. (Millgate 1982, 298)[5]

Gissing certainly would have envied Hardy's opportunities, and thus the aspirations of his male characters are aimed at finding female intelligence as well as beauty. Godwin Peak is probably the best example of Gissing's own frustrated sexual and social desires.[6] In *The Odd Women*, Everard Barfoot also wants an assertive, confident, and educated female companion. Though he has the advantage of social status, his fascination with Rhoda Nunn is largely based on her utter disregard of his class superiority and her insistence on equality both sexually and socially. Compared to Barfoot's liberalism, Jocelyn Pierston, even as a young man, professes an odd kind of romantic conservatism for equality is not one of the qualifications of the well-beloved—in fact, it is a virtual disqualification. Whereas Hardy's hero wants a remote, classical goddess to adore, Gissing's demands an up-to-date one. Significantly, both Pierston and Barfoot possess a certain amount of prestige, and their attitudes toward women are very like students of the sex, surveyors, casual analysts—the artist is devoted to "professional beauty chases" (50) and the intellectual to scrutinizing women's minds. In these two ostensibly dissimilar novels with their opposite-looking male lovers, Hardy and Gissing describe a similar masculine predisposition for sexual fantasy, and the final dissatisfaction with the dream. For these men, abandonment of the ideal stems from both disillusionment with her and from their own frustration at women's independence, or men's growing inability to dominate over the woman they desire. In this respect, Widdowson is as disappointed as Barfoot, and in that character Gissing perfectly illustrates the disintegration of the tyrannical Victorian husband in the decade of New Women.

Hardy and Gissing seem to have felt that however much they might cherish a private fantasy, the "flecked Heroine of reality" was unfortunately destined to persevere. There is something not completely regrettable about her, though. She has a taming influence on men, and Hardy and Gissing, despite fantasies of a fiery romance in their own lives, positively craved a home and felt themselves very much exiled in terms of their background and social status.[7] Thus Pierston feels a very conventional need for a wife. Even in his most passionate pursuits, "he was all the while pining for domestic life" (65), and Barfoot wants to settle down with someone in spite of his revolutionary rhetoric—wants someone, too, who will settle *him* down. He thinks that after marriage to Rhoda their relations will be different for he would "not then be at the mercy of his senses" (268). Thus the ideal is split up even further than her body and her brains, into the evanescent goddess and the good cook.[8] Again, Edward Springrove foreshadows the Hardyan man of the later fiction:

> But the indefinable helpmate to the remoter sides of himself still continued invisible. He grew older, and concluded that the ideas, or rather emotions, which possessed him on the subject, were probably too unreal ever to be found embodied in the flesh of a woman. Thereupon he developed a plan of satisfying his dreams by wandering away to the heroines of poetical imagination, and took no further thought on the earthly realization of his formless desire, in more homely matters satisfying himself with his [affianced] cousin. (*Desperate Remedies*, 201)

Similarly, in *Born in Exile*, Earwaker expresses an urge to divide women into two or more distinct types, which he can manipulate in his imagination but not have to contend with in reality: "For my own part, I am a polygamist; my wives live in literature, and too far asunder to be able to quarrel. Impossible women, but exquisite" (141). Both Earwaker and Springrove, however romantic and escapist, know they can fall back upon a more serviceable, marriageable type of woman to satisfy their need for domestic comfort.

The conventional notion that a man's home is his castle is reassuring for these men, at least in theory. "Traditionally an idea of 'home' has always been one of the key components of British imperialism," explains Andrew Tolson. "For men, this idea was sufficiently flexible to refer to both the immediate nuclear family—the psychological focus of 'manhood'; and to the community, or the nation—the ideological notion of the English gentleman" (1977, 91). For Hardy and Gissing, whose marital home lives were never very happy or satisfying, the sexual wellbeloved must also be an adequate representative of this traditional domestic ideal, a reinforcement of, not a challenge to, masculine superiority. Thus male fantasy, at least in these two novels, is a complex desire for a complex woman whom the lover fails to see as complex—the nymphet and the suffragette, the heroine of the imagination and of the hearth. She is variously condensed into one or the other type in keeping with specific

masculine preferences. It may be without complete and conscious intention that Hardy and Gissing manage to show the
erosion of male fantasy under the press of the hard realities of
women's lives, and how men need to retreat to a safe distance
from their undisciplined "ideal," perhaps settling for less, but
after all feeling settled.

The Well-Beloved is a fanciful novel firmly rooted in a realist
tradition.[9] Even Jocelyn Pierston is anchored to mundane realities despite his romantic inclinations; nothing is more material
than human corporeality, which, for all his "beauty chases,"
Pierston seems to be running from, not seeking. He is rather an
ascetic aesthete: there is a prudishness to his passion, and like
Springrove, he is more sexually alive in his imagination than in
his actual relationships with women. Hardy, however, deliberately obscures this character's sexual history. Unlike Oak and
Winterborne, Pierston is a town man, and supposedly open to
more experiences, or so Mrs. Caro speculates: "He's got lots of
young women, I'll warrant," she tells her daughter (11). But
Pierston's distaste for Avice's ingenuous display of affection indicates otherwise. Indeed, Hardy suggests that part of his discom-
fiture is due to his urbanity. After the spontaneous kiss from a
pretty eighteen-year-old woman, he feels offended instead of
flattered: "But it was so sudden, so unexpected by a man fresh
from towns, that he winced for a moment involuntarily" (10).
Despite his embarrassment, Pierston uses the incident to exercise his masculine prerogative. The fashionable London sculptor
realizes that Avice's sudden consciousness of her womanhood,
her genuine affection, and her shame at her unthinking expression of it, can be used to his advantage. Indeed, the entire
incident "was beginning to be a source of vague pleasure to him"
(12).

The pleasure for Pierston is in his recognition of the power he
has in this relationship, something the dreamy sculptor trans-
lates in his imagination as the return of the well-beloved. Power
is sexually stimulating to Pierston, just as it is with most of
Gissing's men; one thinks not only of Barfoot, but of Hilliard in
Eve's Ransom, who counts entirely upon female gratitude to gain
his advantage. With the first Avice, and even in his subsequent
infatuations, Pierston resembles not only Springrove, but Manston as well, who is attracted to Cytherea Graye partly because
she is his social inferior, and he luxuriates in "making much of
her womanhood, nothing of her situation" (Desperate Remedies,
241).

As much as Pierston would like to isolate Avice's womanhood, he cannot overlook the reality of her situation, her background, and her tastes. Although Avice can recite poetry, play the piano, and sing, Pierston is somewhat edgy about the limited and unexceptional accomplishments of this " 'nice' girl" who is "above all things nice" (19). The imperious goddess, if she exists at all in Avice Caro, is buried under her ordinariness. Avice is almost too tractable:

> He observed that every aim of those who had brought her up had been to get her away mentally as far as possible from her natural and individual life as an inhabitant of a peculiar island: to make her an exact copy of tens of thousands of other people, in whose circumstances there was nothing special, distinctive, or picturesque. (19)

Reality, in terms of quantifiable feminine accomplishments— "the tendency of the age"—intrudes upon a male fantasy that thrives on feminine mystery. Thus the common, knowable Avice is easily eclipsed by the enigmatic female figure on the road with her classical ease and strength, who looks to Pierston "a very Juno." Marcia is at first "a new type altogether in his experience" (23) and different from Avice in every way. Above all, she is independent-minded, proud, and determined, and Pierston cannot resist falling into the dual role of worshipper and rescuer in the perfect accidental tryst. But though Pierston is smitten, the narrator clearly does not wish to present Marcia as being anything near extraordinary, and again Hardy interferes with his hero's romantic imaginings by inserting subtle reminders of petty reality, as in the clipped pairing, "He scented a romance. He handed her five pounds" (24). Money is power, and Pierston has money—something the imperious "Juno" values as she creates her own knight errant, thereby giving away her real childishness and her bourgeois feminine ambition. Hardy makes no effort to disguise the adolescent nature of this romance:

> "Then I have been staying quite near you, Miss Bencombe. My father's is a comparatively humble residence hard by."
> "But he could afford a much bigger one if he chose."
> "You have heard so? I don't know. He doesn't tell me much of his affairs."
> "My father," she burst out suddenly, "is always scolding me for my extravagance! And he has been doing it to-day more than ever. He said I go shopping in town to a simply diabolical extent, and exceed my allowance!" (27)

After Pierston's impulsive marriage proposal, Marcia's first response is, "Will you be a Royal Academician?" (33). Such materialistic concerns give the lie to Pierston's "queenly darling," and the ensuing banalities of their awkward relationship at the inn cause Pierston to once more question the well-beloved. It is embarrassing for a man to find he has betrayed himself in his idealizations, and Pierston "seemed to hear sardonic voices, and laughter in the wind at this development of his little romance" (47).

The most sardonic voice is the narrator's, to be sure, but Hardy also sympathizes with the aging, ardent lover. Past fifty himself, Hardy was aware of the smoldering possibilities of "sleeping fires," to borrow the title of Gissing's novella. Pierston, at thirty-eight, loved "with an ardour—though, it is true, also with a self-control—unknown to him when he was green in judgment" (51). His glimpses of women in omnibuses, cabs, shops, and slums are treated with amused pity, expressed through the warnings of Pierston's friend Alfred Somers, a popular painter who ends up marrying an approximate well-beloved and lives in unimaginative bourgeois comfort. Somers's intrusive realism functions as an authorial check on the infectious fantasies of the protagonist, who, in his Shelleyan idealism, certainly resembles Hardy (Millgate 1982, 329–33). If The Well-Beloved is a "farewell to novel writing"[10] and a move toward poetry in Hardy's career, his hero is not permitted a very bracing or inspiring exit. The conditions of Pierston's fantasy life are almost microcosmic reflections of the larger social conditions of the 1890s for men who could not, without embarrassment, admit their desire for a woman who, practically speaking, no longer exists. Thus the commonplace, "Victorian" docility of Avice is rejected for the modern-spirited Marcia, who subsequently rejects the man who has idealized her because her so-called unconventionality is a risk to her social and moral security: "It is not nice, my living on with you like this" (42). Victorian island girls and New Women are both less than perfect for Pierston, who, in the confusion of his own desires—his "curse"—and the chaos of progressivism in sexual relationships, really requires a feminine blank he can fill in as he pleases. When, years later, he is sure of Avice's death, he has the void he needs. Her permanent inaccessibility makes disappointment in her impossible. The ideal can remain the ideal only if she exists entirely in a man's private imagination.

At forty, Pierston is still regarded by his acquaintances as a young man. He is a Royal Academician, attends dinners in London, and has inherited about eighty thousand pounds to add to the twelve thousand he already possesses from professional sources, which makes him not only an eligible bachelor, but an exceptionally good catch. The flirtation with Mrs. Pine-Avon is therefore conducted from a position of male power although Pierston is cautious about exerting it fully, scrupulously fearful of corrupting her by making declarations he is not quite sure of— in effect, he is the perfect gentleman in this particular affair, and she plays the role of the attractive, prestigious (and slightly desperate) English lady. His brief obsession with Mrs. Pine-Avon is therefore of a very different nature than his passion for Avice II, who does his laundry, polishes his furniture, and—appropriately enough—dusts all his "Venus failures." In London, Pierston is "in constant dread lest he should wrong some woman twice as good as himself by seeming to mean what he fain would mean but could not" (65). But on the Isle of Slingers, he is more lax in his scruples, surrounded as he is by an aura of reverence for Avice I, an atmosphere of sexlessness that is paradoxically charged with eroticism. Invisibility, the disappearance of the threatening female body, has a much greater sexual appeal than, for example, the reality of Nicola Pine-Avon who, after Avice's death, begins to recede even as she becomes tangible: "she became a woman of his acquaintance with no distinctive traits; she seemed to grow material, a superficies of flesh and bone merely, a person of lines and surfaces" (70). She is almost monstrous compared to the dead goddess of his imagination, whose "flesh was absent altogether; it was love rarified and refined to its highest altar. He had felt nothing like it before" (73). Hardy is clearly being ironic in describing the prudishness of his character's passion, but he is also quite seriously showing men's vulnerability to female beauty, which, it seems in Pierston's case, is more alluring when it is out of sight. Away from her in London, Pierston is obsessed with Avice II, "The phantom . . . now grown to be warm flesh and blood, held his mind afar" (83). But Pierston is by no means tormented by sexual desire; his suffering is always abstracted, it is a longing for the soul, not the body, and only partly for the mind. "It was not the flesh; he had never knelt low to that. Not a woman in the world had been ruined by him, though he had been impassioned by so many" (191). Virtuous as Pierston may seem (he does not fall into Hardy's sinful seducer category, for example), Hardy repeatedly censors his idealiza-

tions, tossing in subtle reminders of Avice's flaws, her lack of
education and her social class, her vulgar tastes, and her naivety,
which often verges on stupidity.

Pierston must really struggle to overlook Avice's persistent
habit of being what she *is*, instead of what he has made of her in
his mind. She is "clearly more matter-of-fact, unreflecting, less
cultivated than her mother had been. . . . There was a disappointment in his recognition of this" (81)—just as there was a disappointment in a recognition of her mother's unoriginality.
Pierston's uneasiness is also due to the discrepancies in their age
and social status. That she "was an uneducated laundress, and he
was a sculptor and a Royal Academician, with a fortune and a
reputation" might be a powerful card to play, but "why was it an
unpleasant sensation to him just then to recollect that he was two
score?" (81). A man can be socially powerful but sexually ill-
equipped to compete with even a twenty-three-year-old quar-
ryman, yet he will invariably use what influence he has in order
to gain female submission. In *The Well-Beloved*, Pierston's manipulation of Avice's subservient position as laundress effectively exposes his impulse to exert authority in order to study her
sexually, but the scene is so banal—and especially banal to the
unfantasizing woman—that it comes across as a picture of intentional, almost stubborn, male self-deception. Hardy's ironic tone
is so acute as to give the episode a comic tinge, adding to
Pierston's ridiculousness:

> But after all, it was not the washerwoman that he saw now. In front of
> her, on the surface of her, was shining out that more real, more
> interpenetrating being whom he knew so well! . . .
> He found fault with his linen, and directed that the laundress be
> sent for. . . .
> "About the washing," said the sculptor stiffly, "I am a very par-
> ticular person, and I wish no preparation of lime to be used."
> "I didn't know folks used it," replied the maiden, in a scared and
> reserved tone, without looking at him.
> "That's all right. And then, the mangling smashes the buttons."
> "I haven't got a mangle, sir," she murmured.
> "Ah! That's satisfactory. And I object to so much borax in the
> starch."
> "I don't put any," Avice returned in the same close way; "never
> heard the name o't afore."
> "O I see."
> All this time Pierston was thinking of the girl—or as the scientific

might say, Nature was working her plans for the next generation under the cloak of a dialogue on linen. (89–90)

Despite the boring dialogue and Avice's obvious weak-mindedness, Hardy's ardent lover is smitten. In fact, though he admits she "had apparently nothing beyond sex and prettiness," he feels that "her limitations were largely what he loved her for" (93). Pierston's efforts to persuade himself of this are heroic. He loves her voice but not her discourse (taking special pains that "in catching her voice he might not comprehend her words"); he calls her privately "a chit of a girl," cold and common, "obscure and almost illiterate," yet she is at the same time "the epitome of a whole sex," irradiated "by the beams of his own infatuation." He "beheld her not as she really was, as she was even to himself sometimes" (107). This is Pierston under the curse, when his vision is bedazzled, but even then the reality of Avice's personality and situation is all too clear to him: "It was true that as he studied her he saw defects in addition to her social insufficiencies." Faced with this masculine dilemma—the desire for the female ideal and the intrusiveness of the female reality—the sculptor typically attempts to launch a Pygmalionesque plan that would shape the female raw material into the male ideal: "he could pack her off to school for two or three years, marry her, enlarge her mind by a little travel, and take his chance with the rest" (104).

Perhaps the boldest representation in fiction of this pervasive male fantasy, especially in late-century England, is Gissing's Malkin in *Born in Exile*, whose scheme is to train fourteen-year-old Bella Jacox for womanhood and then reap the rewards. But, "We have heard before of men who waited for girls to grow up," says Earwaker soberly, and the remark suggests Gissing's awareness of the deception inherent in such dreams, however alluring they may appear. In the same way, Hardy's ironic treatment of Pierston's nervous excitement at sharing his London flat with Avice (which is partly protective and fatherly and partly like Nabokov's Humbert Humbert) gives away the male novelist's realistic bias, mainly because nothing much happens in this awkward and erotically charged situation. For example, in a key scene, Avice and Pierston find themselves in his kitchen in the middle of the night when they hear a mousetrap spring, and the potential for an erotic, climactic tryst is undermined by the ridiculousness of the episode and the banal householdry of it.

What is a dull chore to Avice is for Pierston a source of anguish
and embarrassment. His clumsy proposal and her dense indeci-
sion contribute further to a tone of exasperated romanticism
under sordid circumstances, making him seem to himself "the
most lopsided of God's creatures" (131). His final role in the
episode is grimly unromantic, as Pierston returns Avice to her
sluggish and stupid husband and attends the birth of their child,
before his departure for Rome, where—in a wonderfully suggestive phrase—"the quarries of ruins in the Eternal City" re-
mind the sculptor-lover of the "quarries of maiden rock at home"
(140). The spoiled ideal and the unsullied one are in his mind cut
from the same stone.

Hardy's tone is increasingly sympathetic toward the aging protagonist, and indeed the story becomes less comical (though not
completely devoid of Swiftian irony) when we understand that
Pierston is unable "to ossify with the rest of his generation"
(144).[11] Life's lessons are sorrowful to him because he must
admit unavoidable banality into the realm of pure imagination
for Pierston can no longer preserve the undiluted Shellyan vision
of an ideal love. At sixty, he longs for repose, and so his dreams
must become more practical. In fact, the well-beloved is seen
more with a view toward expediency. Pierston "was fully aware
that since his earlier manhood a change had come over his regard
of womankind. Once the individual had been nothing more to
him than the temporary abiding-place of the typical or ideal; now
his heart showed its bent to be a growing fidelity to the specimen,
with all her pathetic flaws of detail; which flaws, so far from
sending him further, increased his tenderness" (143). Upon
seeing "the specimen"—Avice II—at forty, Pierston feels "If he
did not love her as he had done when she was a slim young thing
catching mice in his rooms in London, he could surely be content at his age with comradeship" (145). This is progress of a sort.
It seems for Hardy such realistic resignation is regrettable but
inevitable, and at the very least only mildy traumatic.

Pierston is like Gissing's retired author, Henry Ryecroft, who at
fifty-three still feels eluded by "the old idle dream: balance of
mind and body" (*Private Papers*, 176). He says, "I know just as
little about myself as I do about the Eternal Essence, and I have a
haunting suspicion that I may be a mere automaton, my every
thought and act due to some power which uses and deceives me"
(171). The feeling is not only analogous to Hardy's hero, who
repeatedly feels that his life is manipulated by a capricious
Aphrodite, it is also typical of late-century sensibilities, and the

very root of the modern image of man as caught in a cosmic farce
and constrained by social forces, unknowable to others and lack-
ing self-direction or the mastery of his own desires and motives.
Thus, even though he is "subject to gigantic fantasies still" (151)
and is "the most romantic of lovers" (179), the love song of
Jocelyn Pierston is finally mundane, worn out with disappointment, and conducted by a middle-aged woman with a mind to
matchmaking, who recognizes "the difference between a rich
bird in hand and a young bird in the bush" (155).

Pierston's desire for Avice III, who is forty years younger than
himself, is not even sexual, but solicitous. "Through being a rich
suitor, ideas of beneficence and reparation were retaining him in
the course arranged by her mother" (161). Virtually the entire
courtship is conducted in darkness in order to obscure his features—another odd suggestion of the beauty and beast tale—and
the most promising aspects of Pierston as husband material are
his education, wealth, and reputation, not to mention the fact
that he will probably die soon. Like the well-beloved of his
dreams, he has become the commodity, the acquisition, and
sadly enough, he is his own creator, the object of successful self-
marketing strategies that still fail to make him happy. When
Avice elopes at the last moment, Pierston is almost relieved,
despite his apparent disappointment: "Don't blame them, don't
blame them," he says. "Don't blame her, particularly. She didn't
make the circumstances. I did" (185). The sense of relief is
accompanied by a desire for unconsciousness and release to
"sleep away his tendencies, to make something happen which
would put an end to his bondage to beauty in the ideal" (191). In
this novel, Hardy shows masculine romanticism as truly a bondage and a curse and worse because it is of Pierston's own design,
and in this respect not very different from even Boldwood's fatal
obsession.

Hardy's insistence on "the flecked Heroine of reality," even in
this fairy tale of male idealism, has parallels in Gissing's *Born in
Exile*. There, the men are always disappointed, self-chastising,
and eager for quiet domesticity and normality after their pursuits
of goddesses and angels, who turn out not to be worth the
trouble. Christian Moxey, for instance, has a revelation reminiscent of Arthur Clennam's reunion with Flora Finching in Dickens's *Little Dorrit*—he finally sees the wonderful Mrs. Palmer as
only "any woman among the wealthy vulgar," though (in a key
sentence) "It did not occur to him to lay the fault upon his own
absurd romanticism" (415). Godwin Peak, who declares all his

life he "wanted to win the love of a woman—nothing more," is described by his friend as having "astounding illusions. At fifty,—well, let us say at sixty—you will have a chance of seeing things without those preposterous sexual spectacles" (442). Peak hopes sincerely for a passionless old age.

Both Hardy and Gissing suggest that men who are susceptible to female beauty in the abstract are the victims of their own constructions—like Pierston, they need to adopt "an air of unromantic bufferism." And yet, by doing so, they risk losing whatever pleasures are enjoyed by playing the fool for love. As John Fowles explains in his essay, "Hardy and the Hag," the hell of the deeply feeling sculptor is preferable to "the paradise of being Mr. Alfred Somers, that 'middle-aged family man with spectacles,' painting for 'the furnishing householder through the middling critic'" (41). Yet Hardy keeps intruding on his character's fantasy with banalities and bourgeois preoccupations, barely trying to disguise from the reader what Pierston can hardly disguise from himself—that all the well-beloveds have been either shallow materialists or undistinguished schoolgirls. Whether these male characters idealize a foolish woman or a worthy one seems not to matter much, for they are often more interested in their imaginative rendering of her than in the woman herself. Thus Hardy and Gissing both view the male urge for sexual fantasy with ambivalence: it is alluring, piquant, but almost always self-deceptive. In Everard Barfoot, for example, Gissing looks at the resisting romantic, the man wary of the Emma Bovary complex, who is (supposedly) obstinately realistic in his lovemaking. If Pierston is Hardy's tamed romantic, Barfoot is Gissing's timid one, pursing the well-beloved within a matrix of power and "new ideas," where fantasy is too potentially ruinous to be indulged.

The Odd Women is Gissing's so-called "feminist" novel, though critics have pointed out that its feminism is highly qualified.[12] Indeed, this book about the plight of women contains some of Gissing's most complex and convincing portraits of men. Overall the book is not so much "a study of vulgarism" as it is a study of human potentialities, and though the focus of the novel is female potential in a realistic setting, there emerges a dormant romanticism as well, suppressed by representatives of both sexes, but particularly by the modern male cynic. In Widdowson and Bevis, for example, Gissing describes male fantasies that are mere poses: the emotional blackmail implicit in Widdowson's cliché-ridden courtship of Monica—"I can't live without seeing you," "Why are you so cruel to me," "All your rules shall be mine"—

turns into the more nightmarish cliché of the suffocating middle-class marriage. Equally, Bevis's role as Monica's pseudo-Rodolfe is disappointing, partly because he has not considered the consequences "in making mild love—timorously selfish from the first—to a married woman who took his advances with desperate seriousness," but also because, in a significant phrase that could well function as the banner of most late-century fiction, he lacked "the heroism of moral revolt" (234).

Unlike these men, Everard Barfoot achieves a kind of heroic status in the novel by adventuring in the world of intelligent and economically independent female "revolutionaries," and he escapes from it (with his ego intact) into a more traditionally feminine world of culture, refinement, and submission. His love affair with Rhoda Nunn is as romantic and as erotic as Pierston's sentimental fantasies. Like Pierston, Barfoot conducts his intrigue from a position of social and economic superiority. His female ideal, though, is not girlishness and innocence, nor even perfect beauty, but maturity and intelligence. The narrator even says, "Let beauty perish if it cannot ally itself with mind. . . . For casual amour the odalisque could still prevail with him; but for . . . the durable companionship of man and woman, intellect was the first requirement" (176). This is a far cry from Pierston's dream girl, but it is still a fantasy of feminine perfection—notably, one that matter-of-factly takes into account a man's less spiritual needs by recourse to "the odalisque." Barfoot's ideal may seem sensible, and at thirty-three he is not about to marry a child-bride, but he is still subject to sexual imaginings, the basis of which is always power. Masculine authority, not feminine intelligence, is the true requirement for Barfoot, and his progressivism does not move beyond that firmly conventional patriarchal code. In this respect he is like Widdowson. Rhoda's haughty independent air is as arousing to Barfoot as Monica's initial liberalist speeches are to her husband. Indeed, after one such speech, Widdowson engages in a brief self-flattering dream that is identical to Barfoot's ongoing one: "The marvellous thought of equality between man and wife, that gospel which in far-off days will refashion the world, for an instant smote his imagination and exalted him above his native level" (160). Gissing's rhetoric makes it clear that we are talking about utopia, the fairy tale of sexual equality, and in a sense Barfoot's preoccupation with women's rights, however cynical, is highly quixotic. Oscar Wilde wrote that "The sentimentalist is always a cynic at heart. Indeed, sentimentalism is merely the bank-holiday of cynicism,"[13] and surely Gissing's Everard Barfoot bears this out. If Jocelyn Pierston is the aesthetic sentimentalist turned cynic— the man who kills off his sensuous side because of too many disappointments—Barfoot is the cynic caught in a sentimental intrigue with a woman who is attractive mainly because she is a mysterious variation of his own private idealizations of femininity. Both men engage in erotic, power-based maneuvers with a mixture of cautious self-awareness and passionate recklessness, yet in the end, both retreat from their self-created adventures into the security of sexual conventions, that is, a socially approved marriage with very conventional social and domestic responsibilities.

Marriage is one of the central issues in *The Odd Women*—or, I should say, marriage and its alternatives in the 1890s. Both Rhoda Nunn and Barfoot have idealized versions of what Hardy calls "that homely thing, a satisfactory scheme for the conjunction of the sexes."[14] They begin with a similar premise that marriage should be "an alliance of intellects," but that too often it is for women "a means of support, or something more ignoble still" (38). For men, conventional marriage was paradoxically viewed as both desirable and distasteful—it provided emotional and material sustenance, but as an institution could no longer guarantee masculine authority as more and more men felt intimidated by what had become an increasingly feminized space. Joel Dubbert's interpretation of Henry James's views on marriage operates within a similar masculine matrix of desire and resistance that, I would argue, existed both in England and America in the last two decades of the century. In the past,

> Women had been directed to assume moral leadership, but they were now dominating the lives of their husbands through womanly expectations and restraints. . . . In the nineteenth century, for the American male, love was a denial of masculine power and instinct, a condition of stultifying dependence, in conflict with the masculine mystique. Marriage, then, was a form of death. (1979, 95–96)

Bachelorhood is preferable to the potential emasculation of marriage: Gissing's description of the Peachey household in *In the Year of Jubilee* is the classic negative example, as is the Reardons' marriage in *New Grub Street*. One is reminded of Mr. Overton's (i.e., Butler's) instinctive response to Ernest Pontifex's engagement announcement in *The Way of All Flesh* (written between 1873 and 1884):

I don't know why, but I never have heard of any young man to whom I had become attached was going to get married without hating his intended instinctively, though I had never seen her; I have observed that most bachelors feel the same thing, though we are generally at some pains to hide the fact. *Perhaps it is because we know we ought to have got married ourselves.* (379; my emphasis)

The last remark undermines the misogyny of the earlier one, at least partially, and is a clue, I think, to men's conflicting urges toward the bohemian and the bourgeois, the liberal modern man and the reassuringly authoritarian Victorian one. It is a feeling Butler seems to utter almost in spite of himself.

There is a lot at stake for men who do marry, as Hardy and Gissing understood well enough from their own unhappy marriages. But to remain a bachelor is also risky, socially, sexually, and psychologically. Men like Barfoot, and Harvey Rolfe in *The Whirlpool*, are forced to rationalize their conventionality by calling it something else; though not at all moral entrepreneurs, they like to think of themselves as sexually enlightened, even as socially useful. Indeed, Micklethwaite in *The Odd Women* says straightforwardly, "It is the duty of every man, who has sufficient means, to maintain a wife. The life of unmarried women is a wretched one; every man who is able ought to save one of them from that fate" (93). Though this attitude expresses men's sense of duty and hence of a social and moral burden, it paradoxically gives men a very peculiar power, that of the rescuer, the generous redeemer. Wives should obey their husbands "out of gratitude," says one character in *The Odd Women*. As Andrew Tolson explains, this sense of masculine munificence disguises a reactionary strain.

And one of the more insidious tendencies of the middle-class male is a liberalism which conceals, but in the end reproduces, his traditional power. What might have been a genuine effort at "companionship" is compromised by a new "moralism"—the *gift* of freedom to women. . . . Such "benevolence" fails to take into account the underlying power-structure within which the "gift" is made. It is a claustrophobic, privatized dialogue, where "negotiation" assumes a perpetual momentum, and which is maintained by the couple as an institution. Men hang on to the institution, not simply for chauvinist motives, or because they do not possess the personal courage to change, but because *they cannot foresee a future beyond its determination.* (1977, 119; my emphasis)

Thus despite misogynic rhetoric that attacks marriage (and there is a lot of it in *The Whirlpool*) and that seems the appropriate rejoinder to feminist antimarriage speeches, the capacity of marriage to determine men's futures and cement their traditional power makes it a compelling choice. Even Barfoot's reference to the "casual amour" implicitly suggests a reverence for the opposite—the serious commitment—that nails down the elusive female and makes her knowable, acquirable, and (unlike the odalisque) grateful. Pierston's amorous career, with his absurd and impulsive proposals to four different women he barely knows, exemplifies the conservatism and the need for sexual determination underlying the urgently romantic lover. After all, Pierston wants marriage, not a "new arrangement," such as those proposed to Alma Frothingham by Dymes and Redgrave in *The Whirlpool*.

Barfoot's lovemaking, however, is more cautiously experimental. As a young man, he learned the hard way when a shop-girl named Amy Drake got him alone in the same carriage to London, and as he put it in man-to-man dialogue, "You foresee the end of it" (95). Barfoot and Jude Fawley could compare notes about female rascality, and so could Pierston for that matter. Still, despite his future circumspection in sexual affairs, Barfoot is not unwilling to indulge his almost scientific interest in that feminine anomaly, Miss Rhoda Nunn. His affair is as romantic and as fanciful as Pierston's imaginative amours, but it is of a more intellectual nature, rather like Bloomsbury-type experiments in personal relationships. Gissing seems finally to suggest, though, that however brave and attractive the New Woman may be (and clearly he feels she is potentially ideal), she cannot fulfill men's desires completely if she does not consent to subdue her will to his—a philosophy Havelock Ellis and Grant Allen (writing in the 1890s) would approve of for its irrefutable biological basis.

The struggle of wills is sexually exciting to Barfoot, as it is to Rhoda, and comprises the core of his fantasy, but eventually he retreats (the penultimate chapter is in fact called "Retreat with Honor") when the struggle becomes frighteningly real, that is, when Rhoda becomes an individual living her own life, and not just a woman living out the role Barfoot has carved out for his "unideal ideal." Rhoda is a challenge and a conquest to Barfoot, just as the three Avices represent the prize, the final reward for Pierston, but Barfoot is not about to compromise his masculinity for love or sexual conquest. Indeed, in relating to Micklethwaite the Amy Drake story, he says bitterly, "I have been the victim of this groundless veneration for females" (94). Nevertheless, Barfoot's idealism regarding women is the reverse side of his cynicism. He is motivated by a pursuit for an ideal woman and an ideal relationship, and he is vocal about it, so much so that male sexual idealism becomes one of the controlling themes of The Odd Women; the consecutive climactic chapters in which Barfoot and Rhoda finally confront each other are even called "The Fate of the Ideal" and "The Unideal Tested." In these chapters, the lovers express their passion for one another, but cautiously—they are uncompromisingly self-protective. The New Woman who disdains marriage as bondage finds she needs marriage to ensure male fidelity, and the New Man, who first offered marriage as a test of Rhoda's progressivism, refuses to repeat his offer if matrimony is nothing more to her than insurance. The novel ends with a deadlock that Gissing feels is endemic in modern love.

As a progressive thinker, Barfoot's feminine ideal is the opposite of the mid-Victorian angel in the house:

> A woman with a man's capability of understanding and reasoning; free from superstition, religious or social; far above the ignoble weaknesses which men have been base enough to idealize in her sex. A woman who would scorn the vulgarism of jealousy, and yet know what it is to love. This was asking much of nature and civilization; did he grossly deceive himself in thinking he had found the paragon? (176)

Like Pierston, Barfoot second-guesses the well-beloved for he prefers to cherish the imaginative abstraction rather than risk disillusionment. His whole approach to Rhoda takes the form of a test—not so much a test of her, but of his own standards of the model female, which he does not want to see betrayed by his mistaken passion. Thus his interest in Rhoda develops from playful, condescending scrutiny of a certain interesting but unideal "type" to a dangerously genuine, and often physically and verbally violent, attachment to a woman he admits does not embody his personal fantasy. When he first meets her at his cousin's, Everard "examined Miss Nunn's figure" with "amused approval" (79). Later he analyzes her features with the air of a sexual connoisseur:

> He scrutinized her, at discreet intervals, from head to foot. To Everard, nothing female was alien; woman, merely as woman, interested

him profoundly. And this example of her sex had excited his curiosity in no common degree. His concern with her was purely intellectual; she had no sensual attraction for him, but he longed to see
further into her mind, to probe the sincerity of the motives she
professed, to understand her mechanism, her process of growth.
Hitherto he had enjoyed no opportunity of studying this type. (101)

The male who is the purveyor of patriarchal civilization,
whether the aesthetic specialist like Pierston or the student of
the female "mechanism" like Barfoot, detaches himself from one
of his culture's mysterious creations and measures her against
private and supposedly unique standards of female value, but
these values are really composed largely of the sexual tastes of
the culture. Miss Nunn is, after all, a recognizable product, "a
type," not a freak of femininity. Thus, ironically, it appears that
the male character's conservatism and the inclination for realism
is embedded in his erotic imagination for both the fantasy and
the reality are denied subjectivity, perceived by men as objects,
types, the "products" either of their private dreams or of the
patriarchal society they represent.

It is interesting that both Hardy and Gissing aestheticize the
masculine point of view in these novels. Pierston and Barfoot,
although attentive to female beauty and to women's bodies, are
not primarily interested in sex. Pierston, as we know, has never
"knelt low" to the flesh, and Barfoot convinces himself that his
interest in Rhoda is "purely intellectual." For Gissing's character,
intellectual detachment is protection against the emasculation of
love, a surrendering to the feminine will, just as Pierston's artistic
detachment manages to protect him from the emasculating reality of a sexually powerful "goddess."[15] Barfoot will not put
himself in a position of deference, which he perceives as bygone
courtliness. Even though he refuses to play up to the old forms of
lovemaking and insists upon sexual equality (at least when it's
convenient), Barfoot's rhetoric is replete with assumptions of
masculine authority, and he takes obvious pleasure in holding
Rhoda by force. "Love revives the barbarian; it wouldn't mean
much if it didn't," he says to Rhoda. "In this one respect I
suppose no man, however civilized, would wish the woman he
loves to be his equal. Marriage by capture can't quite be done
away with" (182). One thinks of the Hardyan man—Alec, Troy,
Wildeve, Manston—who waits in ambush for the woman he
loves.

What tortures Barfoot, though, is the idea that he might really be in love, instead of merely amusing himself "in making vigorous love to Miss Nunn, just to prove her sincerity." He tells Micklethwaite that "if she were rich, I think I could do it without scruple" (94). In an interesting reversal from Pierston's experience of seeing the ideal eroded, Barfoot experiences the unideal transformed into something very near perfection, but only very near. Both men witness the ideal in a state of becoming. Where Pierston sees the rare and beautiful woman becoming ordinary, Barfoot watches the ordinary woman grow exceptionally beautiful and uncommon. It is a frightening encroachment upon his fantasy and his emotional independence:

> But if his intellectual sympathy became tinged with passion—and did he discern no possibility of that? An odd thing were he to fall in love with Rhoda Nunn. Hitherto his ideal had been a widely different type of woman; he had demanded rare beauty of face, and the charm of a refined voluptuousness. To be sure, it was but an ideal; no woman that approached it had ever come within his sphere. (130–31)

He goes on to admit that "the dream exercised less power over him" now that his youth was behind him, and the new fantasy, like Pierston's at age sixty, becomes in a way the death of the ideal, that is, a different woman, who will represent not youthful dreams but "the desire of a mature man, strengthened by modern culture and with his senses fairly subordinate to reason" (131).

The subordination of the senses to reason is Barfoot's particular creed, but his "perfect day" with Rhoda at the sea reveals a strong romantic bent—his desire, typical of turn-of-the-century minds, for "An ideal realized. . . . A perfect moment" (258). Barfoot's lapse into romantic dreaminess is partly representative of the impulse for escape and fantasy that dominated the cultural and historical situation. Donald David Stone explains that, "Despite the sense of historical transformation and drift evident in the 1880's, the rise of imperialism, aestheticism, and philosophical solipsism in that decade attests in varying ways to the unwillingness of many Englishmen to face or endure the changing scene about them. The need for realistic solutions was met instead by a number of romantic evasions" (1972, 24–25). A significant aspect of this changing scene was changing sex roles, and some men may have found more serious means of escapism than Barfoot's flirtation with romance, which seems really only self-ironic indulgence in a relaxing dream. "To dwell there together for the rest of our lives would be supreme felicity," he says to Rhoda, pointing to an idyllic seaside cottage. But he immediately undercuts the fantasy by alluding to "the kind of man who would say that," perhaps an unrealistic idiot or a cunning seducer. Rhoda sees through his "fantastic idealism" and at their last meeting in London says, "the perfection of our day was half make-believe. You never loved me with entire sincerity" (327). She is right, and more than she knows, for even Barfoot's "dream" at the sea is an utterly false one—where Rhoda is concerned, he does not crave tranquility. Barfoot's real fantasy is much more violent and anchored in a need for male power. Indeed, as he travels from Seascale to London, he indulges in a fantasy of emotional sadism, imagining Rhoda's suffering and her eventual submission—"She must shed tears before him, declare her spirit worn and subjugated by torment of jealousy and fear. . . . [H]e smiled in anticipation of that hour" (279).

When Gissing gets inside the masculine psyche and permits us to explore the basis of Barfoot's fantasy—power—the vacillation between romance and realism becomes explicit. Ostensibly, Barfoot resists his imagination, scorning dreamy lovers (like Pierston) as emasculated fools. Yet the feminine ideal is intrinsically part of his own experience of reality: he firmly believes in her elusive existence. Though Rhoda disappoints him because she will not submit, he manages to console himself in the thought that she was an imposter, and that the real well-beloved still exists for him:

> Free as he boasted himself from lover's silliness, he had magnified Rhoda's image. She was not the glorious rebel he had pictured. Like any other woman, she mistrusted her love without the sanction of society. Well, that was something relinquished, lost. Marriage would after all be a compromise. He had not found his ideal—though in these days it assuredly existed. (269)

Ironically, Rhoda turns out to be more of a social rebel than even Barfoot, who certainly receives "the sanction of society" when he marries Agnes Brissenden, a woman of wealth and family who is as lovely and as nondescript as the three Avices. He thinks of her, in fact, as a sort of sexual back-up (rather like Mrs. Pine-Avon in *The Well-Beloved*) who "he felt sure, would marry him whenever he chose to ask her and would make one of the best wives conceivable. But of Rhoda Nunn he expected and demanded more than this. She must rise far above the level of ordinary intelligent women" (261). Barfoot lowers his standards with seemingly little remorse—with more like relief, actually, and with "genuine humility" when he realizes that Agnes is not his for the asking. In a reactionary shift, which comes across to the reader as emotional self-protection (the lover on the rebound), Barfoot's admiration turns from the "glorious rebel" to the well-bred conservative. He is attracted now to wealthy and cultured people who "were not in declared revolt against the order of things, religious, ethical, or social" (319).

Both Gissing and Hardy undermine their protagonists in the end by having them opt for sexual and social security, for the constraints of mature realism instead of the liberty of adolescent romance. The decision to conclude *The Well-Beloved* with Pierston's participation in sewage improvement and the installation of home ventilators recalls Gissing's final picture of Barfoot about to "do his duty" (as he ironically writes to Micklethwaite) and marry a woman who is "content with the unopposed right of liberal criticism" and is "never aggressive" (319). Barfoot uneasily consoles himself for losing the more dynamic Rhoda by replacing her with a less troublesome female—another feminine blank, who is only a name throughout the novel, never once fully described, never given a scene, a voice, a personality. If the conventional male role, that is, the Victorian gentleman, with all the psychological baggage germane to the role, the breadwinner, the domestic ruler seems a trap to imaginative men like Barfoot and Pierston, why do they finally prefer that role to unconventional, romantic interpretations of their sexual identities, as passionate lovers, struggling artists, social experimentors, moral entrepreneurs? Their behavior seems to expose an almost instinctive need for protection not from devouring women, but from themselves, sexually, in terms of their desire for a woman, and socially, in terms of their patriarchal heritage, their manhood, their authority. We have seen both effects in Picrston—the suppression of his "curse" which causes so many sleepless nights,[16] his final rage against Avice when she confesses her marriage, and his use of his social position to win a woman's love. Clearly Barfoot's sexual passion frequently verges on violence. Retreat into fantasy, or in Pierston's case, into aestheticism, functions as a kind of purification of male desire.

There is a remarkably frank explanation of the masculine impulse for intentional and self-protective mystification of the feminine in *The Whirlpool*: Harvey Rolfe, one of Gissing's most

exquisite misogynists, does not want to fall in love with Alma
Frothingham. The passage is worth quoting at length:

> Nevertheless, his thoughts were constantly occupied with the girl.
> Her image haunted him; all his manhood was subdued and mocked
> by her scornful witchery. From the infinitudes of reverie, her eyes
> drew near and gazed upon him—eyes gleaming with mischief, keen
> with curiosity; a look now supercilious, now softly submissive; all
> the varieties of expression caught in susceptible moments, and stored
> by a too faithful memory. Her hair, her lips, her neck, grew present to
> him, and lured his fancy with a wanton seduction. In self-defence—
> pathetic stratagem of intellectual man at issue with the flesh—he fell
> back upon the idealism which ever strives to endow a fair woman
> with a beautiful soul; he endeavored to forget her body in con-
> templation of the spiritual excellencies that might lurk behind it.
> (102)

Gissing is making two incisive remarks here about male desire
and the very roots of male fantasy. First, a man's sense of his
"manhood" is easily threatened by what he perceives as female
mischief—that she has aroused his sexual self, made him desire
her, "subdues and mocks" his sense of male superiority and self-
control. Second, his self-defensive stratagem is to idealize her,
spiritualize her. It is a "pathetic stratagem," we must assume,
because to the male imagination, "Woman" is, and has always
been, above all a sexual being, defined first as sexual. Conventional marriage thus sanctifies and domesticates the desire
that seems like "witchery" to men, but there is an important
trade-off. Like their male authors in this case, the heroes of The
Well-Beloved and The Odd Women seem to long for domestic
peace, but they both dread the implicit emasculation and the
somnolent boredom of ordinary married life. "No marriage for
him, in the common understanding of the word. He wanted
neither offspring nor a 'home,'" thinks Barfoot at one point. Yet
his decision to marry Agnes Brissenden certainly seems to guarantee at least a resemblance to the orthodox habits of connubial
life. This understated reversal is a realistic treatment in fiction of
male panic and retreat that, toward the end of the century, appears in science fiction novels like Bram Stoker's Dracula (1898),
and in male fantasy-adventure fiction like H. Rider Haggard's She
(1887) and Kipling's The Light that Failed (1890), books Fraser
Harrison sees as expressing the male fear of "a woman who sees
herself as a whole person, not one who is waiting to be completed by a husband" (124). Certainly the description of Alma

from the male point of view in the passage quoted above has vampirish insinuations—"Her image haunted him," "eyes gleaming with mischief," "lured his fancy with a wanton seduction." Men cannot graciously perform their matrimonial duty when there are these kinds of women at large in society, and so, not surprisingly, they seek less threatening alternatives—the Agnes Brissendens of the world.

If one of the implied authorial questions behind novels such as *Jude the Obscure* and *The Whirlpool* is "What do women want?" the male version seems equally implicit in *The Well-Beloved* and *The Odd Women*: What do men want? What is the nature of their fantasies? In these two novels, masculine fantasy is anything but monolithic; though the hero may covet the ideal woman in his imagination for whatever personal reason—as an innocent beauty or a bold revolutionary—the pluralities of masculinity invade the singleness of the well-beloved. The male imagination confronts the female reality, setting off the deeply internalized sociocultural male desire for both madonna and magdalen, brains and beauty, and for sexual adventure and domestic security. It is a dichtomy Gissing also presents in the ordeal of Harvey Rolfe, which he aptly describes as a choice between "rut and whirlpool," finally preferring the rut. Hardy likewise displays a realistic bias in his reluctance to reward the hero of *The Well-Beloved* with his feminine ideal. Of special importance in these two novels is the question not only of men's conflicting or paradoxical sexual fantasies, but of the degree of men's awareness of the self-defensiveness in their dreams of sexual fulfillment. Quite naturally, one wonders whether Hardy and Gissing are deceiving themselves in their wish for an ideal woman. Ultimately both authors seem to be aware of the futility of wishing for her, even in self-defense. And yet, as imaginative and sensual men who are alert to the changing relations between the sexes and of women's active rebellion, they are touched by the pathos of not wishing at all.

5

The Other Victim: *Jude the Obscure* and *The Whirlpool*

"Of course the book is all contrasts—or was meant to be in its original conception," wrote Hardy of his last novel, significantly identifying the contrasts as being not primarily between Jude and Sue, but within each character: "Jude the saint, Jude the sinner; Sue the pagan, Sue the saint; marriage, no marriage." As successful as the novel is in illustrating this principle of opposition, it is, I think, even more effective as a story of fatal imbalances and extremes. In the same letter to Edmund Gosse quoted above, Hardy described Sue Bridehead's "abnormalism" as consisting of "disproportion."[1] Indeed, disproportion and self-absorption control the lives of the main characters to such an extent that their tragedy lies in their own inability to discover an obscure middle way in a modern world represented by antithetical fronts, each fanatically resisting infiltration by the other.

One representation of the contrasts Hardy was occupied with is revealed in the repeated references to ancient and modern, old world and new world, the former symbolizing stability, the latter chaos. Jude and Sue hang somewhere in between, not firmly anchored. Their nomadic lifestyle signifies a restless questing for some kind of equilibrium or poised stability—both objectively, within their society ("marriage, no marriage"), and subjectively, within themselves, especially in their sexual identities.

Gissing's novel, *The Whirlpool* (1897), published two years after Hardy's, is strikingly like *Jude* in its delineation of contrasts and disproportions. The protagonist, Harvey Rolfe, clings to his books, to ancient history, to masculine common sense in resistance to Alma Frothingham's emotional identity crisis, and her Sue Bridehead-like nervousness. The impression of split perceptions, of civilization and barbarism, a morally clear-cut old world and a morally confused modern one, is everywhere in the novel, provoking the only happy man in the book, Basil Morton, to utter sagely, "Medio tutissimus"—a middle course is best. But for Harvey Rolfe and Hugh Carnaby, and for virtually every man who collides with the feminine, the middle way is impossible. What lies between "rut and whirlpool"—Rolfe's wonderfully apt names for the division he perceives as inherent in modern life— is a void. As in *Jude*, suicidal behavior informs Gissing's work with a sense of the destructiveness of this moral chaos and the unreasonable pressures men (as well as women) place upon themselves to be happy, either in Wessex, where "mutual butchery" is Nature's law, or in London, where Rolfe stands alone "amid a world of cruelties" (384).

That both Hardy and Gissing should feel depressed about their society may be connected to the fact that very little of the world of Victorian optimism, confidently patriarchal, was easily discoverable after 1890, and what remained of it was rather uneasily organized. Feminism had come out of the newpapers and platforms—the public, political realm—and into the private, personal sphere of men's homes, libraries, and offices, the sanctioned spaces of masculinity. Indeed, Phillotson's anguished moan to Sue Bridehead, "What do I care about J. S. Mill? I only want to lead a quiet life," could very well represent the cry of the exhausted male in the mid-1890s. For men like Phillotson and Harvey Rolfe, who feel not only invaded but baffled by independent-minded women, surrender is preferable to combat. There is no battle of wills between the sexes, as in *The Odd Women*, and no sexual coercion (at least not on the part of men), as in *Tess*. Rolfe gives in to what he feels are his wife's neurotic suggestions, pacifying her desires and enduring her emotional swings from self-assertion to submission to self-mortification, with almost stoical patience, craving above all a peaceful household. Jude, too, is heroically unaggressive and indulgent with Sue; we are almost relieved to hear a rare speech of indignation from him: "I've waited with the patience of Job, and I don't see that I've got anything for my self denial," he tells her on one occasion, but more often it is, "My dear one, your happiness is more to me than anything—although we seem to verge on quarrelling so often!— and your will is law to me" (209, 191). But despite their apparent tractability, these male characters are not exactly giving in to feminine aggression. Jude and Rolfe are hardly hen-pecked husbands cowed into submission by argumentative wives. Their way of dealing with women who are seriously confused and struggling with an intense personal need to carve out some place for themselves in their society is to be broadminded, patient, and understanding—in other words, anything but the old-fashioned Victorian tyrant, the man like Phillotson's friend Gillingham, who recommends that Sue "ought to be smacked, and brought to her senses" (185). These modern-minded male protagonists profess their belief in sexual equality, marital independence, and female professionalism. "Do understand and believe me. I don't want to shape you to any model of my own," Rolfe tells Alma before their marriage. "I want you to be your true self, and live the life you are meant for" (118). And Jude, of course, is willing to do whatever Sue wishes, to marry, not to marry, or to marry, but not each other.

Despite the positive implications—men *are* paying attention to what women are feeling—this male martyrdom verges on withdrawal from, not participation in, the reality of women's struggles. Harvey Rolfe, especially, is a weak middle-class man who expresses his dislike for women in general and his exasperation with his wife in particular by avoiding the opposite sex as much as possible. He never imaginatively, sympathetically enters into Alma's terrifyingly empty world; instead he "meditated on Woman" (359), and we can imagine him shaking his head at the riddle. Similarly, for all of Jude's worshipful affection for Sue, there is a sense of baffled condenscension in his attitude toward her. She is always "a riddle to him," "one lovely conundrum"— "essentially large-minded and generous on reflection, despite a previous exercise of those narrow womanly humours on impulse that were necessary to give her sex" (108–9, 134). The female and her problems, so mystifying to the male, must be treated delicately, with reasonableness and patience; her very being is stamped, as Hardy says, "the Weaker" (112). Men must treat her, then, with gentle understanding in order to assure their own sexual survival.

In his discussion of *Jude the Obscure* in *Phoenix*, D. H. Lawrence addresses this problem of men's detachment from women's inner lives by referring to Sue Bridehead's underrated and highly developed individuality:

> Sue had a being, special and beautiful. . . . Why must man be so utterly irreverent, that he approaches each being as if it were a no-being? Why must it be assumed that Sue is an "ordinary" woman—as if such a thing existed? Why must she feel ashamed if she is specialized? . . . She was Sue Bridehead, something very particular. Why was there no place for her?[2]

Sue herself says, "I am not really Mrs. Richard Phillotson, but a woman tossed about, all alone, with aberrant passions, and unaccountable antipathies" (163). The same words could be uttered by Gissing's heroine as she tries to find a place for herself as a free-thinking young woman abroad, as Mrs. Harvey Rolfe in a small house in North Wales, as a professional violinist in London, and as a self-subdued ex-professional, a wife and mother, in the suburbs. These women's experiences are so intense and so personal that they seem neurotic, inconsistent, even cruel from the male point of view. That their nervousness should permeate masculine consciousness is not surprising, especially since men have their own anxieties about changing sexual relations—hence Jude's and especially Rolfe's preoccupation with control, reasonableness, unemotionalism.

The smooth current of institutionalized masculinity itself seems disturbed by women's problems as they are acted out in the private sphere of personal relationships. "You make a personal matter of everything!" cries Jude to Sue at one point in the novel, surprised that she would introduce "personal feeling into mere argument" (122). Perhaps the most intimidating aspect of late-century feminism for men in *Jude* and *The Whirlpool* is precisely this transference by women of abstract political or rhetorical arguments into men's private lives: What *does* J. S. Mill have to do with us? Basil Ransom, the hero of James's *The Bostonians* (1886) makes a similar complaint to Verena Tarrant. "There you are—you women—all over; always meaning yourselves, something personal, and always thinking it is meant by others!" (327). It is baffling to men that women should suddenly have become so serious, so thoughtful, and so personal about social ideas.

For Sue Bridehead, obviously, the personal is political, and she is deadly serious when she applies intellectual arguments to her private world. Alma, too, is vocal about her unconventionality, although, like Sue, she fails to live the revolution. The combination of "sweet reasonableness"—Rolfe's initial impression of Alma—or an intellect that "sparkles like diamonds," as Phillotson describes Sue, and unreasonable eccentricities, "colossal inconsistency," and oversensitivity, makes women appear both strong and vulnerable, sexually attractive and sexually perverse to the men who love them. But the men in *Jude* and *The Whirlpool* learn surprisingly little from women's experiences of the world, even though they are intimate witnesses to a gradual process of self-destruction, which is not at all gender-specific, since not only secondary male characters, but the male protagonists themselves, suffer from morbidity and depression, and even exhibit suicidal tendencies. What is designated as modern confusion or feminine inconsistency—Women's Problems—may be an unconscious appropriation of men's own latent hysteria and social/sexual phobias onto women.

Outwardly it is clear how the essential duality of the world is set up in these two novels. Confusion, a complex civilization, and modernity are identified with women, who, appropriately enough, seem nervous, vain, sexually abnormal, and hysterical; nature, simplicity, rationality, and sanity are masculine attributes. Careful readings of the novels reveal that men, too, are standing on the edge of an emotional void, and need only that feminine push to lose themselves altogether. Jude is no less nervous than Sue, and Rolfe suffers from "neuralsia," though the male response to these modern maladies is not "hysteria," but "common sense." There is a strong sense of emotional repression in Jude and Rolfe, and as I will explain later, Gissing's character succeeds in building a wall around his emotional life that finally imprisons him. In one passage in *Jude*, Hardy appears to regret that men must stifle expressions of emotion: "If [Jude] had been a woman he must have screamed under the nervous tension which he was now undergoing. But that relief being denied to his virility, he clenched his teeth in misery" (102). Men are emotionally disenfranchised because of their "virility," the trap of an essentially male-created, gender-defined personality; and men, besides feeling privately oppressed, are beginning to be openly labelled "the oppressor" by New Women (though as Jude tells Sue, men are also victims of socialized sexual identities). For example, Rolfe constantly blames himself for his lapses from idealized manliness—his lack of discretion, common sense, forcefulness, rationality, and courage. Jude is possibly the most self-doubting, passive man in all of Hardy's novels, whom Arabella calls "a tender-hearted fool" (54). Thus the gender-opposition that is the ostensible thematic base of *Jude the Obscure* and *The Whirlpool*—her irrationality, his common sense, her chaotic modernism, his simplified traditionalism—is really gender-reflection: the female is obviously wilfull, restless, nervous, alienated; she is also vain and sexually manipulative. The male role is an inverted reflection of these feminine traits, an intentional pose of masculine sanity meant to balance feminine panic. This kind of sexual "compensation" is developed at the cost of male sexual identity; the potential self is buried under repression and denials, and periodically exposed in men's bouts of self-questioning and their enervated desire for peace, retreat, "a quiet life."

That the men in *Jude* and *The Whirlpool* should feel so defeated, even victimized, is something of a paradox, for the heroines in these two novels are not aggressive, vampirish feminists (as in some late-nineteenth century novels by men).[3] Ironically, it is Sue's feminine nervousness and sexual weakness that Jude finds intimidating, not her feminist polemics: "Her very helplessness seemed to make her so much stronger than he" (120). It is women's femininity, not their unfeminine aggressiveness, that overcomes male common sense and self-mastery, and the male protagonists in Hardy and Gissing are ambivalent about fighting an enemy who is so charming at the same time she is threatening—indeed, dangerous in her very delightfulness. Sue and Alma are anything but caricatures of draconic New Women. In *Jude* and *The Whirlpool*, woman is not the destroyer of man, but rather *mulier est hominus confusio*—man's confusion, and more than in the biblical sense of woman as man's ruin. She is also the confusion of man's senses, a sweet infection of disorder in the rational masculine world. To confound a man's self-possession and intellectuality, at least in these novels, may also enkindle "a fresh and wild pleasure" (as Jude feels at first for Arabella). The exasperating and devastating Sue Bridehead is above all, to Jude, "sweet Sue." Likewise in *The Whirlpool*, Rolfe is mesmerized by Alma's enticing beauty: "His cheek was not far from hers; the faint perfume floated all about him; he could imagine it the natural fragrance of her hair, of her breath" (121). Rolfe's senses are pleasantly besotted, but such self-forgetting emotion in a man who is "all but despising himself for loving her" (120) feels like intellectual defeat.

This contradictory impression of woman as both the delight and the destroyer of male sexuality is treated in *Jude* and *The Whirlpool* quite unexpressionistically and with very little romance. Alma and Sue are not, say, Oscar Wilde's Salome or Bram Stoker's Lucy Westenra. You do not find in Hardy and Gissing the lyrical ruminations of the patriarch, the kind of puzzling exemplified in these lines from a Frenchman's journal: "Since the apple of Eden . . . woman has always remained man's enigma, his temptation, his hell and his paradise, his dream and his nightmare, his honey and his gall, his rage and his felicity."[4]

Yet, though hardly as poetically phrased, this feeling of confusion is implicit in Jude's and Rolfe's attitudes toward the women in their lives, and it is ubiquitous in late-century masculine identity. Peter Gay explains,

> Attributing to women confusing and contradictory traits, men found to their astonishment that she was at once timid and threatening, desirable and frightening. With time-honored roles of woman under severe pressure, nineteenth-century men indulged in this projective activity more freely and more desperately than ever. (1984, 170)

The projection of masculine sexual uneasiness onto the bewildering beloved is implicit in male characterization in *Jude* and *The Whirlpool*, as I will later illustrate, but what needs to be processed in that projection is some sense of male involvement in female experience. A reader sympathetic to feminist issues would find Jude's story far more positive than Rolfe's, but because of their complex and contradictory desires, the pull between an emotional life and an intellectual life, between new world and old, both men are unable to fulfill themselves sexually, or know themselves completely, or are unable to find that elusive middle way.

There is a scene in Meredith's novel *The Amazing Marriage*, published the same year as *Jude*, in which the "right-minded great lady" Arpington appropriately scolds another sublime Meredithian egoist, Lord Fleetwood, for abandoning his wife after their wedding (although he first takes her to a prize-fight). Lord Fleetwood, loathing himself for the impulsive proposal, not for the subsequent desertion, plays the injured husband, entrapped by his own romanticism. The aristocratic *tête-à-tête* is a biting expose of "New Men":

> Fleetwood . . . betrayed the irritated tyrant ready to decree fire and sword, for the defense or solace of his tender sensibilities. . . .
> "It's a thing to mend as well as one can," Lady Arpington said. "I am not inquisitive: you had your reasons or chose to act without any . . . [H]usband you are, if you married her. We'll leave the husband undiscussed: with this reserve, that it seems to me men are now beginning to play the misunderstood." (283)

Meredith's short lecture from the point of view of the *femme sage* in the novel effectively undermines the much longer meditations of the self-antagonized, rationalizing hero. Hardy and Gissing likewise show the new man "beginning to play the misunderstood," but he is an average middle-class (or *de*-classed) hero, not a spoiled aristocrat. He usually speaks for himself, in a tone that verges on pleading self-pity. In Gissing's novella *Eve's Ransom,* for example, Narramore bemoans the stereotypic image of the innocent maiden and the rapacious suitor: "The day has gone by for a hulking brother to come asking a man about his 'intentions.' As a rule, it's the girl that has intentions. The man is just looking around, anxious to be amiable without making a fool of himself. We're at a great disadvantage" (105). In Hardy, the image of men as victims of their own machinery—that is, patriarchal society's emphasis on success, chivalry, or honor (much like poor Lord Fleetwood's position as a "prisoner of his word")—is early on argued from the male point of view by Henry Knight in *A Pair of Blue Eyes,* only Hardy's third published novel (1873): "I think you will find . . . that in actual life it is merely a matter of instinct with men—this trying to push on. They awake to a recognition that they have, without premeditation, begun to try a little, and they say to themselves, 'Since I have tried thus much, I will try a little more.' They go on because they have begun" (215). *New Grub Street,* of course, is full of men's complaints about unsupportive wives and a soul-murdering society. When his wife suggests that men who fail are men who never struggled to succeed, Edwin Reardon replies, "Darling, they do struggle. But it's as if an ever increasing weight were around their necks; it drags them lower and lower. The world has no pity on a man who can't do or produce something it thinks worth money. . . . Society is as blind and brutal as fate" (230). Jude, too, complains poignantly—and pointedly:

> "Still, Sue, it's no worse for the woman than for the man. That's what some women fail to see, and instead of protesting against the conditions they protest against the man, the other victim; just as a woman in a crowd will abuse the man who crushes against her, when he is only the helpless transmitter of the pressures put upon him." (227)

Hardy's idea of a man unconsciously pushing on—or being pushed on—and Gissing's image of the man who is dragged into an abyss by the weight of "success" are evocative of a great social and economic tide that threatens to overwhelm men's dignity— what Gissing calls in *The Whirlpool* "life at high pressure." As the narrator of *New Grub Street* says resignedly, "A man has no business to fail. . . . Those behind will trample over his body; they can't help it; they themselves are borne onwards by resistless pressure" (290). Men such as Jude and Harvey Rolfe feel this same wave of pressure carrying them into a vortex that is somewhat less economically focused than it is morally and sexually. Their interest in classical subjects, in Latin and Greek history, indicate a need to return to a world that is a bastion of uncorrupted masculinity, a world that is stable, serene, mentally balanced. That Jude is unable to enroll in the university at Christminster is not as important as his finally giving up his scholarly ambitions altogether because he has to support a family. And Rolfe's ultimate breakdown, his final inability to concentrate on his old subjects of study, is blamed on Alma's lack of interest in his intellectual pursuits. He is, paradoxically, distracted by her inattention.

Though the pressures of masculinity as experienced by the protagonists in these two novels are primarily sexual, they are nevertheless related to the pressures experienced by "the misunderstood," and are not by any means isolated from the social problems of the 1890s. In fact, pressures of sex and society are closely identified. Despite the rhetoric of Doom and Fate in both novels, men largely control their own private interpretations of their world, and their anxieties are self-created, as well as externally imposed. In trying to embody a bridge between masculine reason and feminine emotion, male characters erect barriers against their own retreat, blockading the middle way, which can exist neither entirely of intellect nor of sensuality. By assuring their isolation in their own experience of the world, these men see the world itself as split. Even Jude, for all his love, cannot enter into Sue's deepest impressions of life. "Is a woman a thinking unit at all, or a fraction always wanting its integer?" he asks her confusedly. But his implied idea, by contrast, of masculinity as a "unit" is not quite right either. If women's personalities appear fragmented because they are vulnerable to contradictory emotions, men's identities are tense to the breaking point because of the urgent personal need to remain self-protectively whole.

Jude the Obscure and *The Whirlpool* are not only thematically rich and busy with ideas, but grimly expressive of how mid-century notions of masculinity are beginning to erode under the pressure of economic instability, imperialist controversy, and especially feminism. *The Whirlpool*, in particular, comes across as a chronicle of social ills, and incorporates a homicide, three suicides, and one suicide attempt. If *The Whirlpool* seems a chronicle of unhappy men, *Jude* is more like a bleak tapestry of "unhope" (to apply a Hardy neologism), somewhat larger and more suggestive of the past and its unremembered victims. Still,

Hardy's provincial-pastoral is no less turbulent than Gissing's urban gyre. Social confusion—the "whirlpool" life of London, or "the sleep of the spinning top" of Christminster and beyond—infects men's private experiences with women, who often seem the bearers of social chaos. Men, though, baffled themselves by changing ideas of what constitutes masculinity, and by a civilization—that patriarchal creation—that is suddenly seen as chaotically feminine, make a mistake by looking too far opposite to orderly retreat and unemotional tranquility. The male novelist's imposition of contrasts and extremes emphasizes the impossibility of compromise between the sexes. It is sadly meaningful that suicides finally sever the central love relationships of both novels. The "homely thing, a satisfactory scheme for the conjunction of the sexes" that Hardy refers to in the Preface to *Jude*, is defeated by a combination of unpredictable human passions and a callous, inhuman society.

Jude Fawley, Hardy's victim of female perversity, is also the male character most sympathetic to feminine experience—experience that illuminates his own sexual identity by laying a light upon male emotions, not just male sexuality. Jude (and Phillotson, too, for that matter) admits that he knows nothing about women, has hardly given any thought to the feminine point of view, and is as baffled by his own sexual feelings as he is by Sue herself. Jude also knows very little of the world at large, and indeed the locus of his private thoughts and actions is obscurity. He is first a dreamy boy and then a contemplative man who seems to have common human desires that are at once simple and formidable. The Christminster dream is something for Jude to aim at, but his real need is much larger than a knowledge of Latin and Greek: it is "the yearning of his heart to find something to anchor on, to cling to—for some place which he could call admirable" (23). The yearning for an anchor is transferred from the place to a particular person when he sees Sue Bridehead. It is significant that before he even speaks to her, Jude identifies Sue—or the idea of Sue—using the same language he had used to describe Christminster, as "an anchorage for his thoughts" and "a kindly star, an elevating power" (74, 73). He wishes to find a feminine freehold after the alarming affair with Arabella, a sexual initiation that Hardy describes as "a great hitch" interrupting the "gliding and noiseless current of his life" (37), where Jude feels "as if materially, a compelling arm of extraordinary muscular power seized hold of him" that "seemed to care little for his reason and his will, nothing for his so-called elevated intentions, and moved him along." (38–39). With Arabella, he is carried along by sensuality, uprooted from his masculine studies because of this feminine force. Indeed, after his marriage, Jude is rather more psychologically unsettled and emotionally unanchored than he was as a lonely and naive boy. But if Jude is seeking an alternate type of stability in Sue, he is bound to be disappointed, for she is a woman who is "all nervous motion"—in effect, the sexual embodiment of asexual, intellectualized Christminster. The two fantasies of place and person, the world and the woman, are linked almost unconsciously in Jude's imagination. Even as a boy, talking to the carters on the road, he has become so "romantically attached to Christminster that, like a young lover alluding to his mistress, he felt bashful at mentioning its name again" (21). Hardy's language in describing Christminster, Sue, and Jude's impressions of both is likewise remarkably similar and symbolically mixed. If the town is likened to "the stillness of infinite motion—the sleep of the spinning top" (92), Sue is "mobile," of a "nervous temperament" (77), and always "in a trembling state" (77), though she is "of the type dubbed elegant" (73), just as Christminster is apostrophized (and note the feminine pronoun):

> Beautiful city! so venerable, so lovely, so unravaged by the fierce intellectual life of our century, so serene! . . . Her ineffable charm keeps ever calling us to the true goal of all of us, to the ideal, to perfection.[5]

Jude is attracted by the call to "the ideal," but its sources are imperfect. Both the city and the woman turn out to be anything but "unravaged" by the modern world, and there is something pathetic in Jude's locating his desires in a place and a person more corrupted by contemporary life than he thinks. Indeed, there is something ominous in the old carter's description of this "heavenly Jerusalem" at the beginning of the novel: "Yes, 'tis a serious-minded place. Not but there's wenches in the streets o' nights" (22). The association between the intellectual life and the sensual life evoked in terms of a learned city and its wenches is suggestive not only of a Christminster–Sue connection, but of Jude's psychological split, projected onto these two ideals, between spirituality and passion, the "life of constant internal warfare between flesh and spirit" (155) that Jude himself recognizes as his personal battle.

The psychological equation of Christminster and Sue

Bridehead also suggests an artistic attempt to link the central obsessions of the protagonist by using connective symbols and narrative strategies such as foreshadowing—the photograph of Sue, for example, which early in the novel haunts Jude, ultimately forming "a quickening ingredient in his latest intent" to follow Phillotson (63). The implications of the symbolic association of city (intellectual promise) and Sue (sexual promise) become expanded for Jude into the idea of world, of civilization itself, and woman as the representative of the more subliminal forces driving the social machinery. He identifies Sue, in particular, as a product of civilized, modern life, and her nervousness as a symptom of a general social neurosis.

Peter Gay gives a rich treatment of the history of nineteenth-century nervousness in *The Tender Passion*, concluding that "The discovery and promotion of nervousness in the nineteenth century therefore turns out to be largely another eloquent witness to the anxiety that innovation generates" (1986, 349).[6] That Jude's anxiety, his own restlessness, is exacerbated by Sue's innovative morality (partly brought about by his desire for her sexually and her resistance), is another example of his mental association of women and civilization, sex and artificiality, a sophisticated version of Arabella's dimple-making and tail of false hair. The transference of a *zeitgeist* onto women, and onto one woman in particular, operates two ways for Jude: because Sue is so influenced by the modern world, she is not responsible for her perversity, and yet her perversity is what is dragging him back to the barbaric codes of modern life that he disdains. To have Sue is to have in one woman what Basil Ransom in *The Bostonians* identifies as "a feminine, a nervous, hysterical, chattering, canting age" (327); no matter how far Jude and Sue retreat into obscurity, away from the diseases of the age, she will carry with her its whining, womanly, complicated complaints.[7] Like Milton's Satan, which way she flies is Hell: she is herself modernity.

The narrator of Meredith's *The Amazing Marriage* likewise shrewdly comments on men's association of a complex world— or "Life"—with femininity, but in a tone saturated with irony, and so quite different from Hardy's sympathetic portrait of his young hero. Yet the similarities between the intellectual meanderings of the egotistical Lord Fleetwood and the modest, if confused, Jude Fawley (and Gissing's Harvey Rolfe, as well) point to a curious psychological inclination on the part of some late-century males:

Having established Life as the coldly malignant element, which induces to what it chastises, a loathing of womanhood, the deputed Mother of Life, ensues, by natural sequence. And if there be one among women who disturb the serenity we choose to think our due, she wears for us the sinister aspect of a confidential messenger between Nemesis and the Parcae. (368–69)

In Meredith's ironic interpretation, woman is "sinister" because she brings confusion, she disturbs the cultural current. For Jude, the association of woman with a muddled world is so acute, so imbedded in his consciousness, that he really does not know how to distribute the blame for the confusion of his life and the dissembling of his ambitions:

Strange that his first aspiration—towards academical proficiency—had been checked by a woman, and that his second aspiration—towards apostleship—had also been checked by a woman. "Is it," he said, "that women are to blame; or is it the artificial system of things, under which the normal sex-impulses are turned into devilish domestic gins and springes to noose and hold back those who want to progress?" (172–73)

One aspect of *Jude the Obscure* attempts to address this male-centered question, typically general and abstract, by putting it in personal terms. If Sue is, in Jude's eyes, "quite a product of civilisation" and "an urban miss" (111), she is to the narrator also a creature defined by her sex, apart from her socialization:

every face [in Sue's dormitory] bearing the legend "The Weaker" upon it, as the penalty of the sex wherein they were moulded, which by no possible exertion of their willing hearts and abilities could be made strong while the inexorable laws of nature remain what they are. (112)

One would infer that "the inexorable laws of nature" are also responsible for the opportunities afforded or denied to the male sex as well. If she is molded to submission, must he by necessity be molded to aggression? Sue's attempt to explain men to Jude indicates that from her perspective, he is acting in accordance with natural, biological urges: "An average woman is in this superior to an average man—that she never instigates, only responds. . . . Your wickedness was only the natural man's desire to possess the woman" (279). Jude rejects Sue's interpretation of men, because for him the prison of the masculine personality is tied to this very notion of male sexual conquest as detached from feminine sensitivity. He replies to Sue passionately, "You have never loved me as I love you—never—never!" (279). Jude is not crushed psychologically because he wants to possess Sue and cannot, but because he feels her equation of masculine sexual desire and "wickedness" omits the possibility of masculine love, narrowing down complicated sexual and emotional needs to men's "grossness."

Though Jude has always recognized that his interest in Sue was "unmistakably of a sexual kind" (80), he is not a seducer (as he later accuses himself) and not an egoist (like Gissing's Tarrant and Elgar) who is controlled by his sensuality. Even more than sexual satisfaction, Jude wants "something to love." "After all," he says, "it is not altogether an *erotolepsy* that is the matter with me, as at that first time . . . [I]t is partly a wish for intellectual sympathy, and a craving for loving-kindness in my solitude" (80). Though he is rationalizing his "weakness," Jude is able to distinguish between "that first time" with Arabella, which was purely sexual, and a very different feeling of comradeship, affection, and interest combined with sexual attraction that he calls love. Sue's greatest slight to Jude's masculinity, from the masculine point of view, is not that she refuses to give herself to him sexually, but that she initially prohibits him from loving her ("You mustn't love me—you are to like me, that's all") because she associates male love with sexual proprietorship and aggression.

Thus Hardy's most functionally passive man acquires tragic-heroic tones: he blunders toward a selfhood that, in the half-thwarted process of development, is an attempt to redefine his masculinity, to undo the ideology of male sexual dominance, and yet preserve what is truly manly in his sexuality. The love he is able to give to Sue is in his eyes pure, even sacred, and still vaguely linked to his idea of her as a Christ-ministering angel, so to speak, an intellectual and moral guide. Jude tells her fervently, "All that's best and noblest in me loves you, and your freedom from everything that's gross has elevated me" (210). But Sue's obsession with his "natural" desire for sexual penetration, for possession—the same male instinct she fears in her marriage to the anything but lascivious Phillotson—distorts the complex man who is Jude Fawley by focusing on one aspect of him—his sexuality. Jude's "old complaint" is, significantly, not that Sue withholds herself sexually, but that "intimate as they were, he had never once had from her an honest, candid declaration that she loved or could love him" (205).

Sue's fear of being herself confiscated sexually, with which Hardy invites us to sympathize, makes her seem cruel to Jude, who only wants to love her, and be loved by her, the way his "nature," and to some extent his early training with Arabella, encourages a man to love a woman. His generalizations about women and sex in this regard are confused by his confrontations with two particular examples: Arabella provokes his sexuality, and Sue wounds and insults it. Jude feels he is more than a mere cluster of hormonal drives, and also more than a cog in a social machine—more than the "mould civilization fits us into" (163)—and he is striving to synthesize the "natural" man, the sensual, with the "civilized" man. The unbearable irony for Jude is that though he knows he is more than a relative being, defined only by his sexual relationships, the primary referent for his interpretation of society is his sexuality, identified with incoherent emotions and, equally important, with illogical marriage laws.

Indeed, in Jude's mind he is two people: an innocent boy, before the sexual fall, and a postlapsarian sexual adult man. Jude's view of himself as a divided personality is at the source of his masculine identity:

> He could not realize himself. On the old track he seemed to be a boy still, hardly a day older than when he had stood dreaming at the top of that hill, inwardly fired for the first time with ardours for Christminster and scholarship.
> "Yet I am a man," he said. "I have a wife. Moreover, I have arrived at the still riper stage of having disagreed with her, disliked her, had a scuffle with her, and parted from her." (61)

Manhood, for Jude, is closely connected to having a wife, a masculine responsibility that is both public and private. Yet Jude feels he cannot "realize himself" in the role of husband, almost as though his boyhood had been ambushed by his sexual urges. Jude's reflections even as a child indicate a discomfort with the prospect of adulthood: growing up brings oppressive social obligations and confrontations with unharmonious laws of nature. In the same way, Rolfe in The Whirlpool wishes his own son could remain in "the golden age" and be spared the distressing onslaught of sexual appetites. For Jude, adulthood, and especially sexual maturity, incorporates the whirlpool into private existence, even obscure existence:

> All around you there seemed to be something glaring, garish, rattling, and the noises and glares hit upon the little cell called your life, and shook it, and warped it. If he could only prevent himself growing up! He did not want to be a man. (17)

Jude blunders his way through adolescence full of insecurity and self-abasement. Like Rolfe, he feels he is an exile and a misfit, socially inept and constantly risking humiliation. Jude wishes he had not gone to Arabella's, wishes he had not visited Phillotson, wishes he had not written to the college deans. "Well—I'm an outsider to the end of my days!" he sighs (259). The truth of the utterance is borne out in the novel on every page, and yet it is partly true because Jude does not "realize himself" enough to know where he could belong, even if he had the courage, the confidence, or the opportunity to pull down the walls that shut him out.

In trying to make sense of his social and psychological position, Jude embraces the patriarchal authority of ancient civilizations, the mentally balanced and male-defined worlds of Greece and Rome. Unlike Sue, who is "an epicure in emotions" (she admits, "My curiosity to hunt up a new sensation always leads me into these scrapes"), Jude believes in common sense, consistency, rationality, and practicability—a key word for all the characters in the novel, but for Jude a doctrine he repeatedly fails to follow. The hysterical, emotion-oriented female is opposed to the rational male ideal, but however preoccupied Jude is (and Phillotson, too) with practicability and order, he is up against a "chaos of principles" (258) when it comes to society, and against Sue's "extraordinarily compounded" logic (173) when it comes to his personal relationship with a woman. Jude's lapses into irrationality embarrass and virtually emasculate him; that his actions contradict his theories seems an unforgiveable weakness in a man who bemoans his "bygone, wasted, classical days" when abstract authority and personal experience were neatly defined and separate (214). "It would be just one of those cases in which my experiences go contrary to my dogmas," Jude says, regarding the question of Sue's nuptial "duties." "Speaking as an order-loving man—which I hope I am, though fear I am not" (167). Later he announces to the Remembrance Day crowd, "I am in a chaos of principles—groping in the dark—acting by instinct

and not after example" (258). Phillotson also feels the authority
of example is being eroded by his experience with a particular
woman. "O, I am not going to be a philosopher any longer! I only
see what's under my eyes," he tells the matter-of-fact Gillingham
(184). That men's sexual experiences contradict their time-
honored beliefs effectively calls into question the whole notion
of what constitutes authority, and is the closest Jude and Phillotson come to entering into feminist argument, which sees subjective experience, not objective—and here patriarchal—example,
as genuinely authoritative.

The masculine point of view, Jude learns, is only one of several
perspectives. This understanding is a major achievement for any
of Hardy's male characters, and almost an impossible one for a
Gissing protagonist, who, if he does concede something to
female subjectivity, does so with a too self-congratulatory air. It is
true that Jude still tends to see Sue as the sexual other he cannot
quite make out: "Women are different from men in such matters.
Was it that they were, instead of more sensitive, as reputed, more
callous, and less romantic; or were they more heroic?" (140).
Despite his abstraction here, the admission of woman's possible
heroism is an important breakthrough in masculine psychology—it is something, for example, Angel Clare cannot immediately accept in relation to Tess, Troy in relation to Fanny,
Tarrant to Nancy Lord, or Barfoot to Rhoda Nunn.[8] The erosion of
Jude's classical, patriarchal, authoritative ideals is the crack in
his socialized masculinity through which a ray of feminine reality can shine.

If experience can be defined as "an encounter of mind with
world, as a struggle between conscious perceptions and unconscious dilemmas,"[9] then Jude's experience with society and sexuality can be represented by a struggle between old prejudices
and new passions. He tells the Remembrance Day crowd that he
is "a sort of success as a frightful example of what not to do,"
(258) thereby suggesting an awareness of having lived out some
kind of story of development. Of course, one of the greatest
ironies of Jude the Obscure is that the education of the hero
comes at the expense of sacrificing the heroine to a perverse
reactionism. The "death" of Sue Bridehead is comparable to
Alma's drug overdose at the end of The Whirlpool. The world is
too much for these intelligent and sensitive women, who are
without guides or laws or examples—who, in effect, begin by
rejecting patriarchal authorities, and yet find their private experi-

ence tragically complex. At the end of *Jude the Obscure*, the bedridden protagonist summarily says to the widow Edlin,

> "[Sue] was once a woman whose intellect was to mine like a star to a benzoline lamp: who saw all *my* superstitions as cobwebs that she could brush away with a word. Then bitter affliction came to us, and her intellect broke, and she veered round to darkness. Strange difference of sex, that time and circumstance, which enlarge the views of most men, narrow the views of women almost invariably." (317)

The last sentence is a fairly accurate epitaph to this particular novel, for the intrusion of a feminine personality, which itself finally collapses, broadens the sympathies and dispels many of the prejudices of the last of Hardy's fictional heroes. But however much he seems to have grown in self-awareness—"mentally approaching the position which Sue had occupied when he first met her" (245)—Jude is frustrated and destroyed by the impossibility of balancing his private passions with the prohibitions set up by both his society and the progressive antisocial woman he loves, who paradoxically, is identified with Christminster, the laws of civilization, and with the uncivilizing contradictions of her age and of her sex. Wedged between the Arnoldian "two worlds," Jude's growth is in effect the stirring of unfulfillable desires that are the root of his social and sexual identity. Though he aborts his own potential by suicide, Jude's story affirms the mysteriousness of masculinity: the vulnerability he finds inherent in his "natural" virility is an intolerable awareness of an aspect of himself that goes deeper than socialized roles or self-assumed postures of what it means to be a man.

The Whirlpool is comparable to *Jude the Obscure* in that it is about men and women trying to remake themselves, to balance the emotional life and the rational, the private and the public, the ideal old world and the changing new world. Gissing's male submits to the sexual revolution instead of kicking against it, but he does so with a nostalgic resignation that is even more subversive than open rebellion. Jude's life would have seemed a nightmare of sexual awareness to the protagonist of The Whirlpool. Indeed, after reading Hardy's novel, Gissing remarked, "A sad book! Poor Thomas is utterly on the wrong tack, and I fear he will never get back on the right one."[10] The way to deal with feminist reality for Harvey Rolfe is not to accept or sympathize with

female subjectivity, as Jude tries to do, but rather to make a show
of submission, and then retreat to sealed-off, sane, masculine
subjectivity—in other words, to subdue the conflict between the
sexes by ignoring women and couching male sexuality under a
code of common sense. "What a simple matter life would be, but
for women," thinks poor caged-up Hugh Carnaby, expressing
what could well be the grim keynote of The Whirlpool—and
surely there are moments in Jude the Obscure where the same
thought may have occurred to the hero of that novel. But Jude
does not, ever, want to lose touch with Sue's sense of reality,
despite her "cruelty" and her frustrating inconsistency. In contrast, virtually all of Rolfe's actions are motivated by a need to get
further from, not closer to, the woman he supposedly loves. The
only way for a man to survive, Gissing implies, is to stay clear of
females and subdue male sexual instincts, a strategy that has its
own alienating and destructive side effects for men.

Though evocative of a tempestuous open space, the whirlpool
metaphor in Gissing's novel is also an image of stagnation and
enclosure. The genuine growth of the protagonist, Harvey Rolfe,
is impossible because, despite his proclaimed antithesis, "rut
and whirlpool" are the same thing, and are equally destructive.
"Yes, I know it too well, the whirlpool way of life," says Mrs.
Abbott. "I know how easily one is drawn into it. It isn't only idle
people." Rolfe replies, "Of course not. There's the whirlpool of
the furiously busy" (156–7). Inertia and industry are self-reflec-
tive extremes in this novel, and there is no place to live peacefully in between them for nervous people like Harvey and Alma
Rolfe, who exhibit many of the traits exemplified by Jude and
Sue, transplanted to the metropolis. But whereas Hardy's man
emerges with at least a sense of feminine experience, Gissing's
self-occupied, self-protective gentleman remains shut out from
the feverish preoccupations of his wife, never opening himself to
her confused desires, though he imagines he is an irreproachable
modern husband. Gissing appears to want to vindicate Harvey's
masculinity, and the whole novel comes across as a miserable
warning against feminism, imperialism, financial speculation,
modern education, and modern marriage, all of which threaten
masculine peace, dignity, and authority. Indeed, one could apply
any of these themes to a focused analysis of The Whirlpool, not to
mention Gissing's declared intention that the book is about fatherhood.[11]

In Gissing in Context, Adrian Poole makes a compelling claim
for the novel. "The Whirlpool is a parable about the necessary

failure of the dream of perfect autonomy," he says, adding, "It is precisely the impossibility of Rolfe's fiction of perfect separateness that Gissing is intent on disclosing" (1975, 199, 201). To some extent, this is a precise analysis, but there is a subtle and essential distinction between autonomy, which I understand to mean independence or self-containment, and purposeful alienation, the possibly unconscious urge for estrangement between the self and the objective world. Alma, like Sue Bridehead, wants autonomy, to be self-governed, and to create herself fully, not merely to be completed by a husband. Jude, too, in his relationship with Sue, craves perfect separateness based upon equality and mutual respect. Rolfe, however, appears to want sexual insulation, not sexual autonomy. He is preoccupied with a dissociation from the feminine (i.e., public and social) world, but in constructing barriers to block out that part of reality, he also necessarily has to erect barriers to keep intrusive aspects of his own sexual identity (his "baser appetites," for example) out of his conscious—almost ultra-self conscious—role playing.

Indeed, Rolfe is only the central player in a collection of masculine poseurs in this novel, that, for all its antifeminine rhetoric (Halperin rightly calls The Whirlpool, "That most misogynic [sic] of Gissing's novels")[12] seems drained of the attractions of a masculine mystique; it is all machismo, without delivering a convincing impression of masculine strength. The retreat from femininity that informs virtually every chapter is, in effect, men's refusal to look inward and explore their own sexuality. The novel is full of psychologically and emotionally numb male impersonators, among whom Rolfe is the most conspicuously self-deceived; he strolls oblivious and untouchable through a sexual battle zone.

If The Whirlpool is about a man's "process of enlightenment" (Poole 1975, 201) as is Jude in one sense, Poole is correct to emphasize the inconclusiveness of Rolfe's development, which certainly seems suspended between extremes. But if Rolfe is passively arrested in the eye of the hurricane, it is because that is where he wants to be—he is not only unwilling to enter imaginatively into Alma's struggles, but he persistently denies that such struggles exist, both within his wife and especially within himself. He denies or ignores the conflicts that inform his personal existence, wishing to be tepid and undisturbed when what is happening in his marriage is equivalent to Jude's experience of being hit in the ear with a pig's pizzle.

To be sure, Rolfe is an egoist, but he is a unique example in the

Gissing gallery for he is virtually without sexual particularity, merely an assemblage of masculine accoutrements, habits, and tastes, free from what Sue Bridehead would call "grossness." The very quality of virility that defines Tarrant, Elgar, and Barfoot seems unnaturally subdued in Harvey Rolfe. His sensuality is dressed up in the habiliments of the late-Victorian gentleman; he seems empty of passion. Yet this character has Gissing's implicit sympathy for he personifies the almost universal male weariness with the complications and intrigues of sexual awareness.

The narrator introduces Rolfe as a "vigorous example" of a "rational man," whose bent is toward an "indolent conservativism" (20, 2). "I have no opinions," he says, and it is almost his refrain in the novel. "My profound ignorance of everything keeps me in a state of perpetual scepticism. It has its advantages, I dare say" (15). Rolfe's cynicism barely conceals his anxiety, and his "fathomless ignorance" and evasiveness are not policy, but conflict. His curious sexual constraint may be the winding down of virility under feminism. He smugly begins where men like Biffen and Reardon (*New Grub Street*) and Peak (*Born in Exile*) tragically end, with subdued appetites and a personality shut off from the world because of conflicting desires and unfulfilled passions. Unlike these men, Rolfe does not appear to be beaten by anything in particular, and certainly not by any mighty love for a woman. He has "no purpose in life, save that of enjoying himself" (2), and yet he is advertized as the victim of something, at the very least of some harassing self doubts.

Rolfe's cool sexual stoicism is not simple obedience to a bourgeois creed: he is no Giles Winterborne. Instead, Rolfe's sealed-off sexual self is part of a thirty-seven-year-old man's conscientious campaign to sabotage debilitating and uncomfortable emotions— to deny his own sexual "instincts" in the interest of escaping "woman's problems." Ironically, in seeking to live a balanced life, Rolfe removes the counterweight. "There is the humiliating point of our human condition," says the male narrator of *The Amazing Marriage*. "We must have beside us and close beside us the woman we have learned to respect. . . . 'That required other scale of the human balance,' as Woodseer calls her, now that he has got her. . . . We get no balance without her" (561–62). Apparently unconvinced by the Meredithian notion of human fulfillment and sexual equilibrium, Gissing in *The Whirlpool* seems to suggest that in 1897 male survival has come to mean tenacious sexual suppression. This early description of Rolfe's state of mind, for example, is a key passage:

> Not seldom of late had Harvey flattered himself on the growth of intellectual gusto which proceeded in him together with a perceptible decline of baser appetites, so long his torment and his hindrance. His age was now seven-and-thirty; at forty, he might hope to have utterly trodden under foot the instincts at war with mental calm. He saw before him long years of congenial fellowship, of bracing travel, of well-directed studiousness. Let problems of sex and society go hang! He had found a better way. (21)

Rolfe's "better way," however, is not the middle way; it is instead a path of extreme self-protection that is to a large extent based on a fear of women projected onto something much larger and abstract: society. Rolfe's discomfort in London society is caused almost entirely by his uneasiness around women, and is a direct contrast to the reassuring masculine club with which Gissing sets the scene in chapter 1: men smoking cigars, reading newspapers, and drinking brandy, speculating on the economy, and complaining about "domestic management" (6). It is a bastion of masculinity, a place Rolfe retreats to later in the novel with a sense of real urgency, as if he needs to resurrect his sense of sexual superiority. Even Alma says, quite shrewdly, that her husband is a different person after he's been to the club, he displays "a kind of gaiety . . . quite in a boyish way" (172). As the whirlpool—i.e., feminized society—threatens to engulf him,

> as a natural consequence of the feeling of unsettlement, of instability, he had recourse more often than he wished to the old convivial habits, gathering about him once again, at club or restaurant, the kind of society in which he always felt at ease—good, careless, jovial, and often impecunious fellows. (250)

This description complies with John Fowles's view of the Victorian club as an institution that "pandered . . . to the adolescent in man" (*The French Lieutenant's Woman*, 235). It also sounds like the robust equivalent of Alma's recourse—also "more often than [she] wished"—to the "little phial with its draught of oblivion" (307). Indeed, a fascinating aspect of Gissing's conception of this character is that he seems to unconsciously reflect the very neuroses he identifies as feminine: vanity, moral weakness, intellectual inconsistency. Rolfe's instinctive need to preserve his identification with maleness, represented by the club, is a recasting of Alma's strong wish to carve out a place for herself as a professional woman, which seems slightly more understandable, given her position, than her husband's heroic reclusiveness.

"The days are past when a man watched over his wife's coming and going as a matter of course," Rolfe tells Carnaby. "We should only make fools of ourselves if we tried it on. It's the new world, my boy; we live in it, and must make the best of it" (215). Apparently progressive, even optimistic, statements like this— only a sampling of Rolfe's modern-minded rhetoric—conceal a deep feeling of male anxiety and distrustfulness of change; the protagonist has persuaded himself that he is both disinterested, or unbiased, as well as uninterested, indifferent to the new order of sexual relationships. Yet he cannot remain psychologically secure in his self-imposed emotional and intellectual isolation. Even more than poor Jude Fawley, "poor old Rolfe" (Carnaby's tender epithet) is fraught with insecurity; his rational pose is a shield against anything that could threaten his patient stoicism. Indeed, the almost constant refrain of this "rational man" is one of self-reproach for being either too rational, or not rational enough. Clearly, he feels uncertain about his sexual identity and about masculine strength. For example, Rolfe repeatedly chastises his "moral cowardice" (24) yet does not assert himself in even the most trivial situations. He is always embarrassed by his "incorrigible want of tact" (153), a foible that seems only the result of a cultivated insensitivity. Certainly on one occasion, after he hears of Bennett Frothingham's suicide, Rolfe feels slightly abashed at his own coldness:

> It occurred to him that it might be a refreshing and salutary change if for once he found himself involved in the anxieties to which other men were subject; this long exemption and security fostered a too exclusive regard of self, an inaptitude for sympathetic emotion, which he recognized as the defect of his character. (45)

It seems that here we have one of Gissing's egoists on the edge of self-awareness; and yet, Rolfe is always and proudly self-possessed, a quality that "differed little from unconcern," according to the narrator, and that eventually traps him in a manly pose of unruffled practicality that alienates him from the emotional— i.e., "feminine"—side of his personality.

Despite his passivity, Rolfe's essential masculinity is never challenged in the novel. He is clearly "manly" in everyone's eyes, and certainly he cannot be called, as Jude is, "a tender-hearted fool." But if Jude is sensitive to the sufferings of others, craving to give and receive love, he is also passionate and sensual. Rolfe, on the other hand, is neither tender-hearted nor sexually vibrant. He is virtually an ascetic, both emotionally and sexually, and he advertises himself as such ("circumstance" is his god and "common sense" his creed), even though he perceives the falseness in the role he plays. It is as though the mask he purposefully wears to protect himself controls or limits his capacity for self-realization.

Perhaps it is because of his own slender awareness of the duplicity in his nature that Rolfe scorns the vulgar hypocrisies and poses of society. "What a grossly sensual life was masked by their airs and graces," he thinks while noting the women's "unnaturally lustrous" eyes as they return from supper. "He had half a mind to start tomorrow for the Syrian deserts" (41–42). Clearly the impulse to run away is associated not so much with society life as with female sexuality. He hates himself for attending these social affairs, yet there must be a reason he is attracted (sensually) to such "gross" company. Even as Rolfe delivers diatribe after diatribe against women (or, more accurately, drops nasty remarks—"I hate a dirty, lying, incapable creature, that's all, whether man or woman. No doubt they're more common in petticoats"), he must force himself to avert his eyes from Alma Frothingham for "She stood a fascination, an allurement, to his masculine sense" (32). He dislikes this arousal—indeed, he is ashamed to have "yielded to Alma's fascination" (104), feels "more awkward, more foolish" than he has ever felt, and senses that his male superiority and control have been overcome by female "witchery." The only way to domesticate this wild captivation, for Rolfe, is to marry it, and so satisfy an annoying desire in order to get on with more important masculine pursuits. This is, in effect, a practical application of his private law of self-preservation, the "saving strain of practical rationality which had brought him thus far in life without sheer overthrow" (115). He gets very little pleasure from being in love, and seems quite unaffected by the deliciously turbulent emotions that torture men like Tarrant, Elgar, and Peak, or even Alec d'Urberville and Boldwood. He does not wish to see himself as susceptible to desire —in fact, he wishes to be above sexuality altogether. If a man is unfortunate enough to have sexual longings, the logic goes, he must marry at once so he is not unreasonably distracted by them.

Rolfe here is functioning within the popular precinct of the practical man, an immensely attractive image of masculinity at the turn of the century. He is to some extent playing the part of the efficiency man, but surely Rolfe is anything but a "brainworker." He is, rather, an idler who produces nothing, not even an original idea. Gissing's hero has a pretension to H. G. Wells's masculine model, and acts upon Wells's formula for controlling inconvenient sexual impulses by gratifying them: "it is better to marry than to burn, a concession to the flesh necessary to secure efficiency," Wells wrote in 1901.[13] Rolfe applies the efficiency code to a troublesome aspect of himself he hardly wishes to recognize—his sexuality—and then dismisses the tension that precipitates and then succeeds his marriage as not worth any energetic attention: "This was love; but of what quality? He no longer cared, or dared, to analyse it" (113).

Shunning self-analysis, Rolfe refines his power of self-deception. It is interesting to come across the following confession very late in the novel:

> in wooing Alma he had obeyed no dictate of the nobler passion; here, too, as at every other crisis of his life, he had acted on motives which would not bear analysis, so large was the alloy of mere temperament, of weak concession to circumstance. (335)

This seems to be an admission of lust in a man who prides himself on his dispassionate sensibility. It is comparable to Jude's disappointment in being unable to match his actions to his theories. Rolfe at this point is certain that he does not love Alma, and possibly has never loved her; yet as a gentleman, he admits he is partly responsible for their mutual estrangement. This does not, however, from Rolfe's point of view, make his marriage a living hell (though Alma feels her life is "a nightmare"), and it is precisely because "he had no sense of hopeless discord in his wedded life" (335) that he is able to contrive a plan of action that will satisfy his own need to maintain the present situation, and remain as much as possible sealed off from "feminine" activities taking place outside the circle of his private experience. "Love did not enter into the matter; his difficulty called for common sense—for rational methods in behavior towards a wife whom he could still respect" (336). The male character's response to a delicate marital problem—which, in fact, far from being ignored, requires above all a "concession" to love—is typically masculine considering the ideologically dominant equation of manliness and "rational methods" in the 1890s. Rolfe approaches his predicament in "an engineering spirit,"[14] self-centered and male-centered, that almost pathologically shuts out feminine subjective experience. Though we may grant Gissing a sympathetic view of this character, and in fact be willing to recognize the pathos of Rolfe's deeply pessimistic nature, all compassion is eclipsed by the repeated, conscious refusal to acknowledge a version of reality separate from his own, and as tragically legitimate. While his wife is ill with grief over the death of her newborn baby, Rolfe privately philosophizes that it is all for the best, and cannot console Alma because he "feared to seem unfeeling" (393). After her agonized penitent pleas to her husband to believe in her fidelity, and on the very night she kills herself, Rolfe says, "we mustn't talk of it. Sit down and be quiet for a little," and feels "all a man's common-sense in revolt" (447). While she is traumatized by a disastrous sequence of events—not the least of which is a devastating feeling of guilt, plus being witness to a murder—Rolfe "was trying to persuade himself that nothing much of moment had come to pass" (445). Such sensible proceedings expose Rolfe's utter rejection of female subjectivity. He is unable or unwilling to see women's experience as contributing to the same world he inhabits, though at the same time his rationalizations expose a reluctance to admit that his version of man-made reality is not hermetic. Gissing views his character's survival strategy with ambivalence—Rolfe is wrong, for example, to ignore his wife's neurosis, just as he is wrong to suppress his own capacity for emotion. The narrator suggests that Rolfe's temperament, though partly due to personal weakness, is also the product of socialized masculinity, an ideology that teaches men to respect women's tender nature, and under the pose of gentlemanliness encourages men to consider the female's delicate constitution and inferior intellect.

> Rolfe erred once more in preferring to keep silence about difficulties rather than face the unpleasantness of frankly discussing them. . . . Like the majority of good and thoughtful men, he could not weigh his female companion in the balance he found good enough for mortals of his own sex. With a little obtuseness to the "finer" feelings, a little native coarseness in his habits towards women, he would have succeeded vastly better amid the complications of his married life. (365)

In other words, men who cannot apply the same moral standards to both sexes are not wilfully prejudiced, but "good and

thoughtful," misguided and perhaps unable to view women as
equals because society has taught them that women are "the
Weaker." Robert Louis Stevenson was one late-century author
who perceived the dangers for men of an ideology that implicitly
recommends separate codes of ethics for each sex. He prag-
matically advised, "It is better to face the fact, and know, when
you marry, that you take into your life a creature of equal, if of
unlike, frailties; whose weak human heart beats no more tune-
fully than yours" (1906, 36). It does not occur to Rolfe that Alma's
frailties could be anything more than female problems. A confused mix of institutionalized gentlemanliness and his modern
belief in marital independence (the rejection of "the old fash-
ioned authority of husbands") prohibits Rolfe from treating his
wife as an autonomous individual and a social equal for a man
cannot entirely respect what he feels obliged to protect. The
irony is that though he permits his wife to pursue a musical
career and to move freely in society, Rolfe is still susceptible to
sexual prejudices reinforced by patriarchal culture. He is not
above classifying Alma as one of "the brainless number of her
sex" (382). His habitual, almost unconscious, wish to escape
from women thus goes far deeper than his conscious pose as "the
pattern of marital wisdom" (336) and the epitome of modern
masculine open-mindedness. The shaft of feminine—and feminist—experience that found a chink in the shell of Jude's masculinity fails to illuminate the impervious masculinity, itself
pathetically shallow, of Gissing's modern man. But then, as
Henry Knight matter of factly says to Elfride Swancourt in *A Pair
of Blue Eyes*, "Shallowness has this advantage, that you can't be
drowned there" (363).

Gissing appears to grant Rolfe a successful retreat at the end of
The Whirlpool: his wife conveniently dead, he enjoys a smoke
and a philosophical chat about Kipling's *Barrack-Room Ballads*
with the Ryecroftian Basil Morton, and then, "Hand in hand,
each thinking his own thoughts," walks peacefully and manfully
"homeward through the evening sunshine" with his seven-year-
old son (453). It is a patriarchal idyll and smacks of male wish-
fulfilling fantasies. It does, I think, point to Henry Ryecroft's
romance of perfect isolation, but Rolfe's insulation from the sexual traumas that seem to be whirling around him in the "new
world" undermine his situation at the end of the novel. Rolfe's
whirlpool may be shallow, but it is evocative of the feeling Meredith attributes to one of his heroes, an uncomfortable impression of "the bubbling shallowness of the life about him, and the

thought . . . of sinister things below it" (*Beauchamp's Career*, 225). There is no genuine sense of Rolfe's development, self-realization, or "conversion" to a broader understanding of gender-specific experiences, but there is a level of real escape from women. Gissing seems to feel—as *The Private Papers of Henry Ryecroft* (written 1900–1) indicates—that this retreat is in itself cherishable, a positive alternative to the peace Jude achieves at the end of his story, which does free men from "sex and society"—the two myths that have become so inextricable, so intricately entangled and identifiable, in the imaginations of many late-nineteenth-century men.

Conclusion

Hardy's and Gissing's novels point out the ambiguous nature of masculinity with uneasy precision, especially if we compare their novels to those of Dickens, Thackeray, or Trollope. For the mid-Victorian writer, the male *role* was, to a large extent, equated with male *identity*: Mr Harding, in *Barchester Towers*, behaves like a kind-hearted Christian gentleman because that's what he is; Steerforth in *David Copperfield* behaves like a sexually vigorous, high-spirited, and spoiled young man because those attributes make up his real personality. But Gissing's high-spirited, sexually vigorous men in, for example, *The Emancipated*, *In the Year of Jubilee*, and *Born in Exile* are playing a role they cannot quite master. For example, Godwin Peak in *Born in Exile* is a passionate man, like Elgar and Tarrant, who always feels compelled to defend his unruly temperament, as if to persuade himself of it. Compared to, say, Bradley Headstone in *Our Mutual Friend*, whose passionate nature is written in every gesture and in every line of his face, the Gissing man is only a proud, nervous poseur. Similarly, many of Hardy's characters feel the necessity of defining themselves and publicizing their roles. "I'm a bad man," say Alec d'Urberville and Sergeant Troy; "I'm cursed," says Pierston, and they act bad or cursed without culpability, having deterministically stated, "I am what I am" or, more accurately, "I am what I pretend to be."

In emphasizing the difference between the mid-Victorian novelist's description of masculine identity, and Hardy's and Gissing's portraits of masculine roles, it becomes clear that late-century novelists dealt with the complications of character, personality, self, and other in ways different from their predecessors—especially the male self and the female other. More than for Dickens, love and sexual desire are important determinants of masculine self-realization for Hardy and Gissing; certainly sexual relations are central to the thematic implications of the eight novels I have discussed in detail here. A character's attitude toward women in general or one woman in particular is the essential key to unlocking his masculine identity. "If I marry now, it will be a woman of character and brains," says Barfoot in *The Odd Women* (144). Angel Clare says of Tess, "What a fresh and virginal daughter of Nature that milkmaid is!" (176). For each of these men, their feminine ideal is a fairly accurate index to his perception of a counterpart masculine ideal, which, of course, he knows he embodies himself. Barfoot's urbanity and progressivist pose is revealed in his remark, just as Angel's somewhat affected aversion to modern urban life is revealed in his attraction to an innocent, simple country girl. Yet, as I have suggested, neither Barfoot nor Angel Clare really know themselves, nor for that matter do they know Rhoda or Tess, the individual women who are the projections of their fantasies. Angel and Barfoot are two examples of men who misinterpret the identity they have created for themselves. Both characters conceal their basic fear of female autonomy and their conservativism under a modern masculine image. "Man is not what he is, he is what he hides," wrote Andre Malreaux. Often, for the Hardy and Gissing man, what he hides from others is hidden from himself as well.

The patriarchal residue absorbed by Hardy's and Gissing's male characters is revealed subtly enough, even with the accessibility of a new vocabulary and the relatively open debates on sexual topics brought on by turn-of-the-century feminists. In a way, Hardy's and Gissing's novels bridge the Victorian's reticence and the Edwardian's openness about masculine and feminine codes of behavior. By 1925, for example, a best-selling novel, Warwick Deeping's *Sorrell and Son*, can casually make this distinction: "Maurice had ideals; he wanted to think of all women as he thought of his sisters, pale, sweet, Burne-Jonesian, and he was terrified when he saw the Rossetti woman" (244). Such an overt and self-conscious distinction, made by a male author, between two opposite masculine interpretations of women—recognizing, essentially, that the madonna and the magdalen are male-created images—was only conditionally possible for writers of Hardy's and Gissing's generation. Rossetti died in 1882, and Burne-Jones died in 1898. Surely the sensibility of their conceptions of femininity (though largely unproclaimed as opposites except in aesthetic terms), had a strong grip on the psyche of the average Englishman.[1] For example, in his highly popular novel *Trilby* (published in 1894), George du Maurier describes the heroine, Trilby O'Ferrell, in terms of an artistic ideal, but unlike Deeping's narrator, makes no distinction between the Burne-Jonesian angel and the Rossetti demon, rather lumping all statuesque pre-Raphaelite models into one towering image:

Trilby's type would be infinitely more admired now than in the fifties. Her photograph would be in the shop windows. Sir Edward Burne-Jones—if I may make so bold as to say so—would probably have marked her for his own, in spite of her almost too exuberant joyousness and irrepressible vitality. Rossetti might have evolved another new formula from her; Sir John Millais another old one of the kind that is always new and never sates or palls—like Clytie, let us say—ever old and ever new as love itself! (103)

Trilby is a woman of the nineties—goddess-like, sexual, tall (but "not . . . a giantess, by any means . . . about as tall as Miss Ellen Terry," says du Maurier, adding, "and that is a charming height, I think") who is cast in a novel set in the 1850s. George du Maurier obviously prefers the type of female beauty his male contemporaries advertise as the ideal. What he fails to convincingly evoke, however, is the dove and the sorceress—the sweetness and the terror—artists like Rossetti and Millais portray as opposite images of femininity in their paintings, and the anxiety those images arouse in male characters.[2] Hardy and Gissing, on the other hand, with greater sensitivity and awareness, manage to translate this pervasive madonna/magdalen sensibility into their fiction with more complexity and more ambivalence than writers such as du Maurier, Grant Allen, and Kipling, and with less exaggerated or supernatural symbolism than writers like Bram Stoker and H. Rider Haggard. One essential problem Hardy's and Gissing's male characters struggle with—often without ever really understanding the nature of that struggle—is the projection of a split masculine sexual identity of chastity and "experience" onto women.

For example, nothing could be more pernicious and at the same time more pitiful than Reuben Elgar's speech to his wife in defense of his profligacy: it is not infidelity, and it is certainly not love, he says, but satisfying "an ignoble necessity" (*The Emancipated*, 269). To point out the tenacity of Elgar's rationalization as a part of male ideology, we can look to E. M. Forster's Henry Wilcox, in *Howards End* (written twenty years after *The Emancipated*), who genuinely has trouble distinguishing between "unchastity and infidelity" (259). Wilcox's justification of an illicit affair recalls with startling similarity Elgar's speech to his sister, quoted in chapter 2: "You, with your sheltered life, and refined pursuits, and friends, and books, you and your sister, and women like you—I say, how can you guess the temptations that lie round a man?" (245) But Forster, with the irony and sympathetic levelheadedness of a twentieth-century Meredith, points out his character's pitiful self-deception. Wilcox tells Margaret Schlegel, "I have been through hell," but she considers, "A man who has been through hell does not boast of his virility. . . . Henry was anxious to be terrible, but had not got it in him. He was a good average Englishman who had slipped" (246). The role of the virile man is a convenient moral fortress for Forster's character, just as it is for Gissing's. Neither man is really "terrible" in his passion, and yet each honestly believes his immorality may be defended as a fortunate—a manly—fall, a sign of masculine character and feeling. Male rationalization is sincere, but as Forster quietly says in regard to Wilcox's case, "It was not true repentance" (244).

The problem of finding what is true is complicated for male characters by the social edifice of patriarchy, which has used rationalizations like Elgar's and Wilcox's as one of its cornerstones for centuries, and which is built up by the roles I have discussed. The most potent pose of all is one that underlies all the others, and is almost what we mean when we define patriarchy at all, that is, a conviction of male superiority and masculine authority. All of the men in the eight novels I have discussed, with the possible exception of Jude, are convinced of their stability, rightness, stored strength, and moral and intellectual superiority over women, whether couched in a code of gentlemanly honor (Winterborne and Boldwood), virility (Troy, Tarrant, Alec), modernity (Barfoot), or cynicism (Rolfe). It is as though the image of the Victorian patriarch shadows these men's actions and blocks their half-conscious attempts to achieve selfhood. Indeed, certain figures in some of the novels function as reminders of the comparatively less complicated days before New Women and New Morality. Alfred Yule in *New Grub Street* and Edmund Widdowson in *The Odd Women* are two examples of Victorian hangers-on. Yule especially is described as a tyrant, and his meek wife cowers at his morose expression and unreasonable anger (*New Grub Street*, vol. I, chap. 7). In Hardy's novels, Phillotson's friend Gillingham, in *Jude the Obscure*, represents the traditional male point of view: "tighten the reins" is his advice about Sue (290). And the conservative, narrow Mr. Clare in *Tess* certainly has some influence over his unorthodox son—indeed, "despite his own heterodoxy, Angel often felt that he was nearer to his father on the human side than was either of his brethren" (229).

Just as one aspect of masculinity is defined by a character's sense of sexual strength and the notion of masculinity as a positive force in dispensing order, so is another aspect defined by an existential fear of the very power that constitutes manliness for many characters. The burden of power is exposed in a sense of sexual deficiency or degradation such as Jude's battle with the flesh, Boldwood's shame. Samuel Butler's Mr. Overton, for example, is taunted by the girls' chant—"a na-asty bo-o-oy"—but the chief character in *The Way of All Flesh*, Ernest Pontifex, is equally oppressed by an inner self that is struggling to break the husk of strong-armed maleness and priggish British respectability. "The Ernest that dwelt within him" insists:

> "You are surrounded on every side by lies which would deceive the elect, if the elect were not generally so uncommonly wide awake; the self of which you are conscious, your reasoning and reflecting self, will believe these lies and bid you act in accordance with them. This conscious self of yours, Ernest, is a prig begotten of prigs and trained in priggishness; I will not allow it to shape your actions, though it will doubtless shape your words for many years to come. Your papa is not here to beat you now. . . . Obey *me*, your true self, and things will go tolerably well with you, but only listen to that outward and visible old husk of yours which is called your father, and I will rend you in pieces." (158)

"That outward and visible old husk . . . called your father" may be metaphorically translated to the invisible husk of the masculine inheritance of the patriarchal legacy received by Hardy's and Gissing's male characters as well, and that they, too, must peacefully incorporate into the "true self"—the self freed from constraining masculine poses, and not just from temptresses and suffragists, nagging wives or New Women.

Looking at Hardy's and Gissing's novels as imaginative expressions of an ideological crisis—as fictions that document a period of sexual revolution and moral controversy, written by men who participate in that crisis "in cultural predispositions beneath the surface of individual awareness" (Tolson 1977, 14)—we can see that both authors interpret the male experience as something both tense and pliant, splendid and painful. In one sense, the fictional protagonist does honor to a masculine tradition of heroism by assuming a self-mythologizing attitude: the seducer and the gentleman, the romantic and the realist are convenient, durable stereotypes supplied by society. Hardy's and Gissing's characters adopt those roles almost unconsciously in their intense desire to carve out for themselves a viable sexual identity. Though Victorian standards of masculine and feminine behavior have broken down, and indeed modern life is a whirlpool of ideas—a "chaos of principles," in Jude's words—these masculine roles, at least on the surface, are equipped with reassurring guidelines. In an effort to find a masculine identity, which is a complex, persistent part of an individual's personality, these novels show how male characters learn to rehearse a manageable, simplified masculine role, which is expected, socialized, and though connected to temperament, largely disconnected from personality. To adopt George Orwell's wonderful phrase, the face grows to fit the masculine mask: Reuben Elgar, the modern rake, believes in his line of defense; Giles Winterborne has aligned himself honestly to a powerful chivalric tradition; Jocelyn Pierston's romanticism is studied and genuinely troublesome, and he quotes Shelley conscientiously; and Harvey Rolfe's declaration that his god is "circumstance" is made with self-protective sincerity.

It is impossible to know Hardy's and Gissing's strategies or inclinations about their heroes, or how much of their own sexual fears and anxieties went into their fictional characters. But if we follow D. H. Lawrence's rule and first of all trust the tale, it is possible to conclude that for the male protagonist, at least, the sexual role is tense and uncertain, eroded by self-doubts, an intrusive reality, and—not least important—by love.

Oscar Wilde, the prince of poseurs at the end of the century, suggestively and tragically represents the paradoxes involved in image-making in all of his works, but most powerfully in *The Picture of Dorian Gray*, first published in 1890. In that novel, the insouciant Lord Henry Wotton says, "But the bravest man among us is afraid of himself" (41). The role assumed by Hardy's and Gissing's man may be partly a self-protective strategy motivated by a fear of himself. But paradoxically, the role that protects his masculinity often blocks the possibility of discovering the best aspects of the inner male self, the individual complex man. Even if it seems that the masculine mask remains intact—as it does for the survivors in these novels, for Angel Clare, Tarrant, Pierston, Barfoot, and Rolfe—there is always the risk that the essential man, as in *The Picture of Dorian Gray*, will wither within.

Notes

Chapter 1. Masculine Identities

1. Fraser Harrison, *The Dark Angel* (New York: Universe Books, 1978), 72.
2. The Act of 1883 enters into the drama of Gissing's *New Grub Street*. After divorcing her husband Edwin, Amy Reardon benefits from the new law and exclaims, "What a splendid Act of Parliament that is! The only one worth anything that I ever heard of" (392). Some men, of course, would have a different opinion about the law. John Galsworthy's *The Man of Property* (1906)—the first in the Forsyte Saga—is a silver spoon novel much concerned with the transition from Victorian earnestness to newfangled Edwardian notions about marriage and sexuality (the novel begins in the year 1886). One male character wistfully recalls the "golden age before the Married Women's Property Act" when he was able to marry "a good deal of money, of which . . . he had mercifully been enabled to make a successful use" (18).
3. See especially Ronald Pearsall, *The Worm in the Bud* (Toronto: Macmillan, 1969); Eric Trudgill, *Madonnas and Magdalens* (New York: Holmes-Meier, 1976); and Steven Marcus, *The Other Victorians* (New York: Bantam, 1966); also Harrison's *The Dark Angel*; Jeffrey Weeks, *Sex, Politics, and Society* (London: Longman, 1981); and Peter Gay, *The Bourgeois Experience* (2 vols.).
4. Andrew Tolson, *The Limits of Masculinity* (New York: Harper & Rowe, 1977), 141.
5. Marcus, *The Other Victorians*, 28.
6. Butler, *The Way of All Flesh*, 276–77.
7. John Halperin, *Gissing: A Life in Books* (Oxford: Oxford UP, 1982), 136–37.
8. David Pugh, *Sons of Liberty* (Westport, Conn.: Greenwood Press, 1983), xv.
9. Jonathan Rose, *The Edwardian Temperament* (Athens: Ohio University Press, 1986), 74.
10. Norman Vance, *Sinews of the Spirit* (Cambridge: Cambridge University Press, 1985), 17.
11. Walter Houghton, *The Victorian Frame of Mind* (New Haven: Yale University Press, 1957), 366.
12. Declan Kiberd, *Men and Feminism in Modern Literature* (New York: St. Martin's Press, 1985), xi and 33.
13. See Penny Boumelha, *Thomas Hardy and Women* (Harvester Press, 1982) chap. 4; and Fraser Harrison, chap. 7.
14. Bruce Woodcock, *Male Mythologies: John Fowles and Masculinity* (Harvester Press, 1984), 89.

Chapter 2. Nasty Boys: *The Emancipated* and *In the Year of Jubilee*

1. "For writers of Gissing's generation—and Meredith, born nearly thirty years before Gissing, lived to become a member of that generation in the eighties and nineties—the relationship between form and feeling has reached a stage of acute crisis. The imbalance was indeed becoming almost intolerable between an expanding interior world of consciousness, of complex, delicate sensitivities and velleities, and an apparently narrowing and rigidifying external world of peremptory self-assertion. It is no wonder that these years produced so many versions of a sharp polarisation between will, success, vulgarity, and pragmatism on the one hand, and will-lessness, failure, imagination and self-consciousness on the other. The keen dichotomies bear witness to an unprecedented anxiety about the relationship between Self and Other." Poole, *Gissing in Context*, 20–21.

2. *The Woman Who Did*, 165.

3. Bristed is quoted by Gordon Haight, "Male Chastity in the Nineteenth Century," *Contemporary Review* (November 1971): 257.

4. Jude tells Sue, "it is no worse for the woman than for the man. That's what some women fail to see, and instead of protesting against the conditions they protest against the man, the other victim; just as a woman in a crowd will abuse the man who crushes against her, when he is only the helpless transmitter of the pressure put upon him" (V, iv). The rustics make the same complaint about unfairly vociferous women at the agricultural fair in *Madding Crowd*, chap. L. See chapter 5 for a fuller treatment of men's sense of their victimization in *Jude* and *The Whirlpool*.

5. Grant Allen, "Plain Words on the Woman Question," *Fortnightly Review* (October 1889): 452.

6. Cf. Sergeant Troy's remark in *Madding Crowd*: "Perhaps in setting a gin I have caught myself" (139), and Jude's feeling of "being caught in a gin which would cripple him" (52). Ian Ousby interprets the remark as one of unconscious irony, even of prophecy: "His pose as susceptible man whose life could easily be ruined by Bathsheba's pretty face is soon no longer going to be a pose. After his marriage he soon feels himself humiliatingly enslaved." "Love-Hate Relations in Hardy: Bathsheba, Hardy, and the Men in *FFMC*," *The Cambridge Quarterly*, X (1981): 37.

7. "When Gissing has Laurence get rid of Philip Vanstone [in the short story "All for Love"], he manifests a temperamental tendency to violence coexisting in him with a reluctance to resort to physical strength, a trait which such friends of his as Morley Roberts, H. G. Wells, and Henry Hick stigmatized as muscular cowardliness. Like many shy individuals whose patience is tried to the breaking point, he would dream of removing the obstacles in his way by violent means. . . . His urge to strike out at insolent or idiotic people when he was exasperated found its outlet in writing." Pierre Coustillas, "Introduction," in *George Gissing: Essays and Fiction* (Baltimore. Johns Hopkins Press, 1970), 33.

8. A discussion of men's anxiety about venereal disease is Elaine Showalter's "Syphilis, Sexuality, and the Fiction of the Fin de Siècle," in *Sex, Politics, and Science in the Nineteenth-Century Novel*, ed. Ruth Bernard Yeazell (Baltimore: Johns Hopkins Press, 1985), 88–115.

9. The significance of R. L. Stevenson's novel is supported by Richard

Ellmann: "The implication of the esthetes' conception of the artistic personality is that a man is really two men. There is the insignificant man who is *given*, whether by God, by society, or simply by birth; there is the significant man who is *made* by the first. One evidence of this split, which goes beyond literature, is the verbal distinction that becomes common towards the end of the nineteenth century between personality and character, the former as in some way the conscious product of the latter. In literature the splitting up of the mind into two parts is accomplished near the end of the century by two books, *Dr. Jekyll and Mr. Hyde* (1885) and *The Picture of Dorian Gray* (1890)." *Yeats: The Man and the Masks*, 72.

10. "There is now to come the new day, when we are beings each of us, fulfilled in difference. The man is pure man, the woman pure woman, they are perfectly polarised. But there is no longer any of the horrible merging, mingling self-abnegation of love. There is only the pure duality of polarisation, each one free from any contamination of the other." Lawrence, *Women in Love*, 193.

Chapter 3. Pathological Gentlemen: *Far from the Madding Crowd* and *The Woodlanders*

1. See Guerard, *Thomas Hardy: The Novels and Stories* (Cambridge: Harvard University Press, 1949), 115–16.

2. Quoted in Mark Girouard, *The Return to Camelot: Chivalry and the English Gentleman* (New Haven: Yale University Press, 1981), 198.

3. "A Chat with the Author of 'Tess,'" *Black and White* (27 August 1892). Quoted in Merryn Williams, *Women in the English Novel 1800–1900* (New York: St. Martin's Press, 1984), 28.

4. *Tess*, 338. Cf. Jude, who after his disillusionment with the possibilities of Christminster and the collapse of his dreams, feels an "awakening to a sense of his own limitations" (94).

5. Clym Yeobright in *The Return of the Native* is an odd example of the gentleman-type in Hardy, perhaps because he is the only protagonist in the major novels whose chivalry is directed toward his mother, rather than his lover—a large part of his gentlemanliness is filial duty. Diggory Venn in that novel belongs to the Gabriel Oak school of devotion without self-deprecation, but he does share with Boldwood and Winterborne, as well as with Oak, a clumsy, rustic chivalry that is both attractive and slightly ridiculous.

6. For more on the passive "New Man" in fiction see Kiberd, especially chap. 1.

7. Cf. Millgate's biography, 279: "Bowker's reference to such figures as 'walking,' as self-propelled, stresses the passivity of the artist throughout the process and coincides with Hardy's own insistence upon the extent to which his characters shaped their own destinies."

8. The similarity between Angel Clare and Henry Knight has been pointed out by various critics. The earlier character almost seems to be a rough draft of the later one. See Millgate's biography, 296–98.

9. For a different reading of Oak as "blustering browbeater" see Rosemarie Morgan, 43–57.

10. See Susan Beegel's essay, "Bathsheba's Lovers: Male Sexuality in *FFMC*," in *Sexuality and Victorian Literature*, ed. Don Richard Cox (Knoxville: University of Tennessee Press, 1984). Beegel claims that the language of love in this

novel is work, pointing out the male sexual symbolism in the tools of Gabriel Oak's various trades.

Chapter 4. Modern Romantics: *The Well-Beloved* and *The Odd Women*

1. Millgate, *Thomas Hardy*, 324; letter to Bertz, 144.
2. Stone, *Novelists in a Changing World: Meredith, James, and the Transformation of English Fiction in the 1880s* (Cambridge: Harvard UP, 1972), 51.
3. "Hardy and the Hag," in *Thomas Hardy After Fifty Years*, ed. Lance St. John Butler (Totowa, N.J.: Rowman and Littlefield, 1977), 41.
4. *The Culture of Narcissism* (New York: Norton, 1978), 324.
5. Though I prefer not to stress speculations on a writer's sexual life, in this instance both men's positions regarding women are interesting informants of their fiction.
6. See John Halperin's *Gissing: A Life in Books*, 159: "Gissing told Bertz plainly that 'Peak is myself—one phase of myself.' " He added: " 'Born in Exile' was a book I *had* to write." Halperin also says the novel "was Gissing's fullest expression to date . . . of his 'exile' philosophy."
7. Stone classifies Dickens, Eliot, Thackeray, Meredith, and Trollope as "outsiders . . . yet, paradoxically, we look to them for a depiction of Victorian equilibrium and to their late novels for an account of the dangers of modern materialism and egoism" (33). See also J. Hillis Miller, *The Form of Victorian Fiction*.
8. The desire for sexual splendor and the need for a good supper seem to be equal concerns for some male artists. In 1849, Charlotte Brontë accuses the ultimate creator, Milton, of a clouded—and middle-class—male imagination in the case of Eve: "Milton tried to see the first woman," says Shirley Keeldar, "but he saw her not. . . . It was his cook that he saw" (*Shirley*, 320).
9. In my discussion I am concentrating on Hardy's final revision of the serial, published in book form in 1897. There are significant alterations. For an excellent comparison of the two versions, see the Appendix to *The Well-Beloved* (Oxford, 1986), edited by Tom Hetherington.
10. See Helmut E. Gerber, "Hardy's *The Well-Beloved* as a Comment on the Well-Despised," *English Language Notes* (September 1963): 52; also *Thomas Hardy: A Critical Biography* (1955) by Evelyn Hardy, 258–60.
11. Cf. the hero of *The Whirlpool*, Harvey Rolfe, who at age forty-two says, "It's bad for a man when he *can't* mature—which is my case. I seem to be as far from it as ever. Seriously, I should think few men ever had so slow a development. I don't stagnate: there's always movement; but—putting aside the religious question—my stage at present is yours twenty years ago. . . . If I had my rights, I should live to about a hundred and twenty, and go on ripening to the end. That would be a fair proportion" (327).
12. For discussions of *The Odd Women's* antifeminism, see Lloyd Fernando (chap. 5) and Kathleen Blake (chap. 4).
13. The quote is from *De Profundis*, in *De Profundis and Other Writings*, 200.
14. From Hardy's essay "The Tree of Knowledge," cited in the Norton Critical Edition of *Jude the Obscure*, 352.
15. In *Trilby*, George du Maurier's 1894 best-seller, the heroine, with her goddess-like stature, models for artists in the Latin Quarter and becomes the

mesmerized singing protegée of the villain, Svengali. Though she seems passive in both roles—as artist's model and as hypnotized artist—Nina Auerbach points out that Trilby's "transforming presence" destroys both Little Billee, the great painter, and Svengali, the great musician. In a way, Trilby resembles the unsophisticated but disruptive Avice. "In drawing on ideals of the alluring vacuum of the uncultured woman waiting for the artist-male to fill her, du Maurier imagines powers that dwarf male gestures toward redemption and damnation." See "Magi and Maidens: The Romance of the Victorian Freud," in *Writing and Sexual Difference*, ed. Elizabeth Abel (University of Chicago Press, 1982), 111–30.

16. "Before I tell you what has happened to me," Pierston said, "I want to let you know the manner of man I am."
"Lord—I know already."
"No, you don't. It is a sort of thing one doesn't like to talk of. I lie awake at night thinking about it. . . . I am under a curious curse." (35)

Pierston's strange confession to Somers early in *The Well-Beloved* has a suggestion of criminality about it, and may be symptomatic of the Victorian fear of masturbation, which was indeed a moral crime. Adolescent boys were frightened into purity by grotesque stories (supposedly medically valid) of the disease, disfigurement, and insanity caused by onanism. The confession of Henry Jekyll in *Dr. Jekyll and Mr. Hyde* carries even more sinister innuendo: "I have brought on myself a punishment and a danger that I cannot name. . . . I could not think that this earth contained a place for sufferings and terrors so unmanning" (74). When his experiments become addictive, he is shocked to find that he "had gone to bed Henry Jekyll and . . . had awakened Edward Hyde"—perhaps indicative of male anxiety about going to bed at night and giving in to corrosive and vile temptations. For a thorough documentation of masturbation anxiety in nineteenth-century England see Ronald Pearsall, *The Worm in the Bud: The World of Victorian Sexuality* (Toronto: Macmillan, 1969).

Chapter 5. The Other Victim: *Jude the Obscure* and *The Whirlpool*

1. Quoted in the Norton Critical Edition of *Jude the Obscure* (1978), 349–50.
2. *Phoenix*, 510. Though Lawrence sounds gentle enough in this passage from *Phoenix*, he is finally alienated from Sue Bridehead's neurotic frigidity. An interesting defense of Sue's sexuality that responds to Lawrence's criticism is Mary Jacobus, "Sue the Obscure," *Essays in Criticism*, 25.3 (1975).
3. Peter Gay meticulously documents the history of the *femme fatale*, the vampire-woman, and the unappealing man-woman in nineteenth-century imagination in *The Education of the Senses*, chap. 2, especially pp. 197–213.
4. Quoted from a journal entry by Henri-Frederic Amiel (1849) by Peter Gay in *The Education of the Senses*, 170. Gay sees the ideas expressed by Amiel as characteristic of his time and class.
5. "The words quoted appear in the preface to Matthew Arnold's *Essays in Criticism: First Series* (1865)." Norton Critical Edition of *Jude*, fn. p. 66.
6. See also Sigmund Freud's essay, "Civilized Sexual Morality and Modern Nervous Illness," published in 1908. Freud cites three psychosociologists, Erb,

Benswanger, and Von Krafft-Ebing, who each published essays (in 1893, 1896, and 1895, respectively) on the subject of "neurasthenia," an illness that they found to be almost epidemic, and caused primarily by the conditions of modern life. Freud finds the epidemic to be (not surprisingly) caused by the "harmful suppression of the sexual life of civilized peoples (or classes) through the 'civilized' sexual morality prevalent in them." One can imagine an eager, but perhaps reductive, Freudian analysis of the main players in *Jude* based on this essay alone.

7. In their feminist study of fin-de-siècle and modernist literature, *No Man's Land*, Gilbert and Gubar suggest that in *The Bostonians* James "depicted the escalation in the battle of the sexes that marked the progress of the nineteenth century," and that he did so with acute paranoia (26; see especially chap. 3). James's novel offers some contrasts between the feminist movement in Great Britain and America from the male novelist's point of view. James's Olive Chancellor and Verena Tarrant are certainly more committed to "the cause" of female emancipation than are Sue Bridehead and Alma Frothingham, for example. But, oddly enough, Jude and Rolfe seem more enlightened about feminist issues and less confident about their masculine prerogative than the closed-minded hero of *The Bostonians*, who faces whole parlors of vocal emancipationists. Perhaps because Hardy and Gissing did not, in *Jude* and *The Whirlpool*, set out to tackle The Woman Question directly, their male characters seem much less combatant and far more confused—the battle lines are not clearly drawn.

8. Rosemarie Morgan argues that Hardy has always sided with his heroines, and that "[f]or all his sympathies with the underprivileged male characters," Hardy finally "treats them with antipathy" as representatives of the status quo. *Women and Sexuality in the Novels of Thomas Hardy*, 162. Morgan's view is compelling, although I see Hardy's treatment of male characters as ambivalent rather than antipathetic.

9. Gay, *Education of the Senses*, 171.

10. Letter to Henry Hick, 29 Nov. 1895, quoted by Morley Roberts, *Henry Maitland*, chap. v. My source is Pierre Coustillas, "Some Unpublished Letters from Gissing to Hardy," *English Literature in Transition*, 1966, 208.

11. Gissing told Morley Roberts that Harvey Rolfe "would probably never have developed at all after a certain stage but for the curious change wrought in his views and sentiments by the fact of his becoming a father." Gissing also wrote to Bertz that in the novel "much stress is laid upon the question of *children*." See Halperin, *Gissing: A Life in Books*, 235 and 242. Interestingly, Gissing made the same claim for *The Whirlpool* to Hardy: "One theme I have in mind—if ever I can get again to a solid book—which I want to treat very seriously. It is the question of a parent's responsibility. This has been forced upon me by the fact that I myself have a little boy, growing out of his infancy." Coustillas, "Some Unpublished Letters . . . ." (dated 3 Sept. 1895), p. 203. Full treatment of Gissing's commitment to the fatherhood theme is beyond the scope of this discussion, but it is certainly relevant that both Hardy and Gissing expressed concern over the inherent morbidity and weakness of the next generation of men, represented by Little Father Time in *Jude the Obscure* and by little Hughie in *The Whirlpool*, with his pale cheeks, his "nervous tendencies," his "too intelligent face" (383, 451). Both novels also touch on men's personal and social responsibilities as parents. Jude, for example, sees "The beggarly question of parentage" as the "excessive regard of parents for their own children,

and their dislike of other people's . . . like class-feeling, patriotism, save-your-own-soul-ism, and other virtues, a mean exclusiveness as bottom" (217).

12. Halperin, *George Gissing: A Life in Books*, 240.

13. In *Anticipations*. Quoted in Jonathan Rose, *The Edwardian Temperament*, 142.

14. The apt phrase is from Rose, *The Edwardian Temperament*, 142. His chapter on "The Efficiency Men," though not particularly a study of socialized masculinity, is a fairly good analysis of the social mood in which Gissing's character frequently operates.

Conclusion

1. By the turn of the century, images of women seem to have multiplied in complex ways. In *Sexual Anarchy*, Elaine Showalter describes how science, as well as art, influenced men's attitudes towards women, who are dissected as case studies "to be incisively opened, analyzed, and reassembled by the male writer" (128), or, conversely, hidden behind veils as the inscrutable Female whose power lies in her mystery. Likewise, Bram Dijkstra, in *Idols of Perversity: Fantasies of Feminine Evil in Fin-de-Siècle Culture*, accounts for an "iconography of misogyny," from the cult of the "household nun" to the vampire woman and the decapitating seductress. The paintings Dijkstra has chosen to reproduce in the book are fascinating and persuasive, as are his selected discussions of social and scientific treatises about women and sex. The reading of *Trilby* is enlightening ("a purification of male brains through feminine sacrifice"), as are his frequent allusions to Zola's amazing heroines. Occasionally, though, Dijkstra makes a speculative leap when he assumes that the male novelist would naturally absorb the culture's misogyny. In *Jude the Obscure*, for example, Sue Bridehead tells Jude, "Until [a woman] says by a look 'come on' [a man] is always afraid to." Dijkstra concludes: "In other words, a woman who was raped wanted to be raped. Hardy knew this was true because science had proved it to be true" (103). Rather narrow, considering Hardy's extremely sensitive portrayal of a rape victim in *Tess of the d'Urbervilles*.

2. For an illustrated discussion of sexuality and pre-Raphaelite art, see Jan Marsh, *Pre-Raphaelite Women: Images of Femininity in Pre-Raphaelite Art* (London: Wiedenfeld and Nicolson, 1987). Also, in her essay, "Magi and Maidens: The Romance of the Victorian Freud," Nina Auerbach points out that du Maurier's huge, vital heroine is the quintessence of overpowering womanhood, who "awes and destroys both hero and villain" (116). Trilby's "seemingly boundless capacity for mutability" makes the sweet uncultured bohemian as dangerous as Bram Stoker's Lucy Westenra.

Works Cited

Allen, Grant. *The Woman Who Did.* 1895. Reprint. London: Grant Richards, 1908.

———. "Plain Words on the Woman Question." *Fortnightly Review.* 1 October 1889: 448–58.

Auerbach, Nina. "Magi and Maidens: The Romance of the Victorian Freud." *Writing and Sexual Difference.* Ed. Elizabeth Abel. Chicago: University of Chicago Press, 1982.

Barker-Benfield, G. J. *The Horrors of the Half-Known Life: Male Attitudes Towards Women and Sexuality in Nineteenth-Century America.* New York: Harper and Rowe, 1976.

———. "The Spermatic Economy: A Nineteenth-Century View of Sexuality." *The American Family in Social-Historical Perspective.* Edited by Michael Gordon. New York: St. Martin's Press, 1978.

Beegel, Susan. "Bathsheba's Lovers: Male Sexuality in *Far from the Madding Crowd.*" *Sexuality and Victorian Literature.* Edited by Donald Richard Cox. Knoxville: University of Tennessee Press, 1984.

Blake, Kathleen. *Love and the Woman Question in Victorian Literature: The Art of Self-Postponement.* Brighton: Harvester Press, 1983.

Boumelha, Penny. *Thomas Hardy and Women: Sexual Ideology and Narrative Form.* Brighton: Harvester Press, 1982.

Brontë, Charlotte. *Shirley.* 1849. Reprint. New York: Oxford, 1981.

Butler, Samuel. *The Way of All Flesh.* 1903. Reprint. London: Grant Richards, 1908.

Cockshut, A. O. J. *Man and Woman: A Study of Love and the Novel, 1740–1940.* New York: Oxford University Press, 1978.

Coustillas, Pierre, ed. *George Gissing: Essays and Fiction.* Baltimore: Johns Hopkins University Press, 1970.

———. "Some Unpublished Letters from Gissing to Hardy." *English Literature in Transition* 9.4 (1966): 197–209.

Deeping, Warwick. *Sorrell and Son.* 1925. Reprint. New York: Penguin, 1984.

Dijkstra, Bram. *Idols of Perversity: Fantasies of Feminine Evil in Fin-de-Siècle Culture.* New York: Oxford University Press, 1986.

Dubbert, Joel. *A Man's Place: Masculinity in Transition.* Englewood Cliffs, N.J.: Prentice-Hall, 1979.

Du Maurier, George. *Trilby.* New York: Harper and Brothers, 1894.

Eliot, George. *Middlemarch.* New York: Norton Critical Edition, 1977.

Ellmann, Richard. *Yeats: The Man and the Mask.* New York: Dutton, 1948.

Fernando, Lloyd. *"New Women" in the Late Victorian Novel.* University Park: Penn State University Press, 1977.

Forster, E. M. *Howards End.* New York: Vintage, 1921.

Fowles, John. *The French Lieutenant's Woman.* New York: Signet, 1969.

———. "Hardy and the Hag." *Thomas Hardy After Fifty Years.* Edited by Lance St. John Butler. Totowa, N.J.: Rowman and Littlefield, 1977.

Galsworthy, John. *The Man of Property.* 1906. Reprint. New York: Charles Scribner's Sons, 1969.

Gay, Peter. *Education of the Senses.* Vol. 1 of *The Bourgeois Experience: Victoria to Freud.* New York: Oxford University Press, 1984.

———. *The Tender Passion.* Vol. 2 of *The Bourgeois Experience: Victoria to Freud.* New York: Oxford University Press, 1986.

Gerber, Helmut E. "Hardy's *The Well-Beloved* as a Comment on the Well-Despised." *English Language Notes* 1.1. (1963): 48–53.

Gilbert, Sandra M., and Susan Gubar. *The War of the Words.* Vol. 1 of *No Man's Land: The Place of the Woman Writer in the Twentieth Century.* New Haven: Yale University Press, 1988.

Girouard, Mark. *The Return to Camelot: Chivalry and the English Gentleman.* New Haven: Yale University Press, 1981.

Gissing, George. *The Emancipated.* 1890. Reprint. London: Hogarth, 1985.

———. *New Grub Street.* 1891. Reprint. New York: Penguin, 1980.

———. *Born in Exile.* 1892. Reprint. London: Hogarth, 1985.

———. *The Odd Women.* 1893. New York: Norton, 1977.

———. *In the Year of Jubilee.* 1894. Reprint. London: Hogarth, 1987.

———. *Eve's Ransom.* 1895. Reprint. New York: Dover, 1980.

———. *Sleeping Fires.* 1895. Reprint. Lincoln: University of Nebraska Press, 1988.

———. *The Whirlpool.* 1897. Reprint. Brighton: Harvester Press, 1984.

———. *The Private Papers of Henry Ryecroft.* 1903. Reprint. New York: Dutton, 1927.

Goode, John. *George Gissing: Ideology and Fiction.* New York: Barnes and Noble, 1978.

Guerard, Albert. *Thomas Hardy: The Novels and Stories.* Cambridge: Harvard University Press, 1949.

Haight, Gordon. "Male Chastity in the Nineteenth Century." *Contemporary Review* 219.1270 (1971): 252–62.

Halperin, John. *Gissing: A Life in Books.* New York: Oxford University Press, 1982.

Hardy, Florence Emily. *The Life of Thomas Hardy 1840–1928.* London: Macmillan, 1962.

Hardy, Thomas. *Desperate Remedies.* 1871. Reprint. New York: Macmillan, 1976.

———. *A Pair of Blue Eyes.* 1873. Reprint. New York: Penguin, 1986.

———. *Far from the Madding Crowd.* 1874. Reprint. New York: Norton, 1986.

———. *The Trumpet-Major.* 1880. Reprint. London: Macmillan, 1985.

———. *The Woodlanders.* 1887. Reprint. New York: Penguin, 1981.

——. *Tess of the d'Urbervilles*. 1891. Reprint. New York: Penguin, 1982.

——. *Jude the Obscure*. 1895. Reprint. New York: Norton, 1986.

——. *The Well-Beloved*. 1897. Reprint. New York: Oxford, 1986.

Harrison, Fraser. *The Dark Angel: Aspects of Victorian Sexuality*. New York: Universe Books, 1978.

Houghton, Walter. *The Victorian Frame of Mind*. New Haven: Yale University Press, 1957.

Jacobus, Mary. "Sue the Obscure." *Essays in Criticism* 25.3 (1975): 304–28.

James, Henry. *The Bostonians*. 1886. Reprint. New York: Penguin, 1987.

Kiberd, Declan. *Men and Feminism in Modern Literature*. New York: St. Martin's Press, 1985.

Korg, Jacob. *George Gissing: A Critical Biography*. Seattle: University of Washington Press, 1963.

Lasch, Christopher. *The Culture of Narcissism*. New York: Norton, 1978.

Lawrence, D. H. *Women in Love*. 1921. Reprint. New York: Penguin, 1984.

——. *Phoenix: The Posthumous Papers of D. H. Lawrence*. Edited by Edward D. MacDonald. London: William Heinemann, 1936.

Lucas, John. *The Literature of Change: Studies in the Nineteenth-Century Provincial Novel*. Brighton: Harvester Press, 1977.

Mangan, J. A., and James Walvin, eds. *Manliness and Morality: Middle-class Masculinity in Britain and America, 1800–1940*. Manchester: University of Manchester Press, 1987.

Marcus, Steven. *The Other Victorians*. New York: Bantam, 1964.

Marsh, Jan. *Pre-Raphaelite Women: Images of Femininity in Pre-Raphaelite Art*. London: Wiedenfeld & Nicolson, 1987.

Meredith, George. *Beauchamp's Career*. 1876. Reprint. Oxford: Oxford University Press, 1988.

——. *The Egoist*. 1879. Reprint. New York: Norton, 1979.

——. *Diana of the Crossways*. 1885. Reprint. New York: Modern Library, n.d.

——. *The Amazing Marriage*. 1895. Reprint. New York: Scribner's, 1909.

Milberg-Kaye, Ruth. *Thomas Hardy: Myths of Sexuality*. New York: The John Jay Press, 1983.

Miller, J. Hillis. *The Form of Victorian Fiction*. Cleveland: Arete Press, 1979.

Millgate, Michael. *Thomas Hardy: His Career as a Novelist*. New York: Random House, 1971.

——. *Thomas Hardy: A Biography*. New York: Oxford University Press, 1982.

Morgan, Rosemarie. *Women and Sexuality in the Novels of Thomas Hardy*. London: Routledge, 1988.

Ousby, Ian. "Love-Hate Relations in Hardy: Bathsheba, Hardy, and the Men in *Far from the Madding Crowd*." *The Cambridge Quarterly* 10.1 (1981): 24–40.

Pearsall, Ronald. *The Worm in the Bud: The World of Victorian Sexuality*. Toronto: Macmillan, 1969.

Poole, Adrian. *Gissing in Context*. Totowa, N.J.: Rowman & Littlefield, 1975.

Pugh, David. *Sons of Liberty: The Masculine Mind in Nineteenth-Century America*. Westport, Conn.: Greenwood Press, 1983.

Richard, Jeffrey. " 'Passing the Love of Women': Manly Love and Victorian Society." *Manliness and Morality: Middle-class Masculinity in Britain and America, 1800–1940.* Edited by J. A. Mangan and James Walvin. Manchester: University of Manchester Press, 1987.

Rose, Jonathan. *The Edwardian Temperament.* Athens: Ohio University Press, 1986.

Showalter, Elaine. "Syphilis, Sexuality, and the Fiction of the Fin de Siècle." *Sex, Politics, and Science in the Nineteenth-Century Novel.* Edited by Ruth Bernard Yeazall. Baltimore: Johns Hopkins University Press, 1985.

———. *Sexual Anarchy: Gender and Culture at the Fin de Siècle.* New York: Viking Penguin, 1990.

Stevenson, Robert Louis. *Dr. Jekyll and Mr. Hyde.* 1886. Reprint. New York: Signet, 1987.

———. *Virginibus Puerisque and Other Papers.* New York: Charles Scribner's Sons, 1906.

Stoker, Bram. *Dracula.* 1897. Reprint. New York: Dell, 1978.

Stone, Donald David. *Novelists in a Changing World: Meredith, James, and the Transformation of English Fiction in the 1880s.* Cambridge: Harvard University Press, 1972.

Tolson, Andrew. *The Limits of Masculinity: Male Identity & the Liberated Woman.* New York: Harper & Rowe, 1977.

Trudgill, Eric. *Madonnas and Magdalens.* New York: Holmes & Meier, 1976.

Vance, Norman. *The Sinews of the Spirit: The Ideal of Christian Manliness in Victorian Literature and Religious Thought.* Cambridge: Cambridge University Press, 1985.

Weeks, Jeffrey. *Sex, Politics, and Society: The Regulation of Sexuality Since 1800.* London: Longman, 1981.

Wilde, Oscar. *The Picture of Dorian Gray.* 1891. Reprint. New York: Penguin, 1988.

———. *De Profundis and Other Writings.* New York: Penguin, 1984.

Williams, Merryn. "Hardy and the Woman Question." *Thomas Hardy Annual no. 1.* Edited by Norman Page. London, 1982.

Woodcock, Bruce. *Male Mythologies: John Fowles and Masculinity.* Brighton: Harvester Press, 1984.

Young, Arthur C., ed. *The Letters of George Gissing to Eduard Bertz, 1887–1903.* New Brunswick, N.J.: Rutgers University Press, 1961.

Index

Acton, William, 22, 24
Adam Bede (Eliot), 27, 34
Allen, Grant, 26, 33, 34–35, 43, 45, 56, 94, 132
Amazing Marriage, The (Meredith), 20, 108–9, 113–14, 122

Barnaby Rudge (Dickens), 27
Beauchamp's Career (Meredith), 39
Born in Exile, 46, 53, 79, 81, 87, 89–90, 122, 130
Bostonians, The (James), 105, 113
Burne-Jones, Edward, 131–32
Butler, Samuel, 22–23, 27–28, 134

David Copperfield (Dickens), 27, 34, 78
Desperate Remedies, 55, 78, 81–82
Diana of the Crossways (Meredith), 68, 69–70
Dickens, Charles, 24, 27, 28, 130
Dr. Jekyll and Mr. Hyde (Stevenson), 52, 140 n.16
Du Maurier, George, 26, 131–32

Egoist, The (Meredith), 29, 39, 42, 44
Eliot, George, 27–28
Ellis, Havelock, 24, 45, 94
Emancipated, The, 16, 18, 29–44, 132–33
Eve's Ransom, 53, 82, 109

Far from the Madding Crowd, 16, 33–35, 51, 55–68, 70–71
Forster, E. M., 23, 132–33
Fowles, John, 30, 77, 90, 123
French Lieutenant's Woman, The (Fowles), 30–31, 52

Gissing, George: as late-Victorian novelist, 14–15, 20, 26–28, 76, 130; and male characters, 26–27, 134–35; and women, 22, 25, 40, 78–79. Works: *Born in Exile*, 46, 53, 79, 81, 87, 89–90, 122, 130; *The Emancipated*, 16, 18, 29–44, 132–33; *Eve's Ransom*, 53, 82, 109; *In the Year of Jubilee*, 16, 18, 27, 29–35, 44–54; *New Grub Street*, 53, 109, 122, 133, 136 n.2; *The Odd Women*, 15, 17, 20, 343, 70, 76–82, 90–100, 131; *The Private Papers of Henry Ryecroft*, 53, 59, 88–89, 128–29; *Sleeping Fires*, 44, 68–69, 74; *The Whirlpool*, 27, 31, 53, 99–101, 102–11, 119–29

Haggard, H. Rider, 15, 26, 100, 132
Hardy, Thomas: as late-Victorian novelist, 14–15, 20, 26–28, 76, 130; and male characters, 26–27, 134–35; and women, 29, 61, 79–80. Works: *Desperate Remedies*, 55, 78, 81–82; *Far from the Madding Crowd*, 16, 33, 34–35, 51, 55–68, 70–71; *Jude the Obscure*, 17, 34–35, 50, 102–19; *The Mayor of Casterbridge*, 36; *A Pair of Blue Eyes*, 55, 109, 128; *The Return of the Native*, 138 n.5; *Tess of the d'Urbervilles*, 27, 31–35, 37, 47, 51–52, 57–59, 131, 133; *The Trumpet-Major*, 27; *The Well-Beloved*, 17–18, 76–90, 99; *The Woodlanders*, 16, 34, 42, 51, 55–62, 70–75
Howards End (Forster), 132–33

In the Year of Jubilee, 16, 18, 27, 29–35, 44–54

James, Henry, 105
Jude the Obscure, 17, 34–35, 50, 102–19

147

Kipling, Rudyard, 15, 26, 100, 132

Lawrence, D. H., 23, 26, 44, 53, 104
Little Dorrit (Dickens), 89
Love: in *Jude the Obscure*, 115–16

Marriage, 92; in *In the Year of Jubilee*,
  50–51; in *The Odd Women*, 80–81,
  92, 94; in *The Well-Beloved*, 80
Masculinity: and chivalric code, 24,
  55–62, 73; and doctrine of experience, 23–24, 33–34, 37–40; and
  feminism, 25, 78–79; and male
  roles, 16–18, 22–29, 133–35; and
  male sexuality, 22–28, 30–35, 52–
  54, 126, 131–33, 134, 140 n.16; and
  patriarchy, 21–22, 133–34; Victorian construction of, 21–28; and virility, 24–25, 31–36, 43–45, 54, 132–
  33
Mayor of Casterbridge, The, 36
Meredith, George, 20, 26, 29, 39, 68,
  108–9, 113–14, 122, 128–29

New Grub Street, 53, 109, 122, 133,
  136 n.2

Odd Women, The, 15, 17, 20, 34, 70,
  76–82, 90–100, 131
Our Mutual Friend (Dickens), 130

Pair of Blue Eyes, A, 55, 109, 128

Picture of Dorian Gray, The (Wilde),
  135
Private Papers of Henry Ryecroft, The,
  53, 59, 88–89, 128–29

Return of the Native, The, 138 n.5
Rossetti, Dante Gabriel, 131–32

Sleeping Fires, 44, 68–69, 74
Sorrell and Son (Deeping), 131
Stevenson, Robert Louis, 15, 128
Stoker, Bram, 15, 100, 107, 132,
  142 n.2

Tess of the d'Urbervilles, 27, 31–35,
  37, 47, 51–52, 57–59, 131, 133
Trilby (du Maurier), 26, 131–32,
  139 n.15, 142 n.2
Trumpet-Major, The, 27

Way of All Flesh, The (Butler), 22, 27–
  28, 92–93, 134
Well-Beloved, The, 17–18, 76–90, 99
Wells, H. G., 36, 126
Whirlpool, The, 27, 31, 53, 99–101,
  102–11, 119–29
Wilde, Oscar, 91, 107, 135
Woman Who Did, The (Allen), 43–44
Women in Love (Lawrence), 44, 53
Women's Movement, 16, 19, 25, 31,
  41, 60
Woodlanders, The, 16, 34, 42, 51, 55–
  62, 70–75